English Skills 3

Answers

Carol Matchett

Schofield & Sims

WHICH BOOK?

The **English Skills** books are aligned with the end-of-year objectives for Key Stage 2. For the majority of pupils aged 7 to 11, follow the guidance given on page 2 as to which book to use with each year group.

If a pupil is working significantly above or below the standard normally expected for his or her age, another book may be more appropriate. If you are not sure which to choose, two simple **Entry tests** are available to help you identify the book that is best suited to the pupil's abilities. You can also use these resources with new pupils joining your class or school.

Photocopy masters of the **Entry tests** are provided in the teacher's guide – which also contains the **Entry test marking keys**, full instructions for use, and a range of other **English Skills** copymasters, including **Diagnostic checks**, which help to identify topics that pupils may be struggling with. The **Diagnostic check marking keys** provide catch-up activities for each topic, in the form of activity prompts, to help secure pupils' knowledge. For ordering details, see page 46.

You may be using **English Skills** at Key Stage 3 or with other mixed-ability groups of young people or adults. In such cases you will find the **Entry tests** vital in deciding which book to give each student.

Published by **Schofield & Sims Ltd**, Dogley Mill, Fenay Bridge, Huddersfield HD8 0NQ, UK
Telephone 01484 607080
www.schofieldandsims.co.uk

This edition copyright © Schofield & Sims Ltd, 2017
First edition published in 2011

Author: **Carol Matchett**
Carol Matchett has asserted her moral right under the Copyright, Designs and Patents Act, 1988, to be identified as the author of this work.

British Library Cataloguing in Publication Data
A catalogue record for this book is available from the British Library.

Design by **Ledgard Jepson Ltd**
Front cover design by **Peter Grundy**
Printed in the UK by **Page Bros (Norwich) Ltd**

ISBN 978 07217 1409 7

CONTENTS

Introduction

Schofield & Sims English Skills provides regular and carefully graded practice in key literacy skills. It is designed for use alongside your existing English lessons, embedding key aspects of grammar, sentence structure, punctuation and spelling and constantly revisiting them until they become automatic. At the same time, it reinforces and develops pupils' knowledge of word structure and vocabulary.

Each pupil book comprises three sections with 12 tests in each one. The tests become more difficult, but the increase in difficulty is gradual. The pupil books are fully compatible with the Key Stage 2 National Curriculum, and the final tests in each book are aligned with the end-of-year objectives as follows:

- **Introductory Book:** Years 1 and 2 (Bridge to lower KS2)
- **Book 1:** Year 3
- **Book 2:** Year 4
- **Book 3:** Years 4 and 5 (Bridge to upper KS2)
- **Book 4:** Year 5
- **Book 5:** Year 6
- **Book 6:** Years 6 and 7 (Bridge to KS3)

Parts A, B and C

Each test is divided into three parts:

- Part A: **Warm-up** – puzzles, 'warm-up' exercises and revision of earlier learning
- Part B: **Word work** – spelling, word structure, exploring words and their meanings to help develop vocabulary
- Part C: **Sentence work** – constructing and punctuating sentences; using words from different word classes; understanding tense, verb forms and other aspects of grammar.

Answering the test questions

After you have demonstrated to the class how some of the different question types are to be answered, the pupils work through the test items without adult help – either individually or in pairs. Encourage them to refer to dictionaries, thesauruses and other appropriate reference materials rather than asking for your help. The tests may be used flexibly. For example, a test may be tackled in one session or over several days.

Marking

This book provides correct answers for **English Skills 3**; where various different answers would be acceptable, an example is provided. The **Focus** panel stating the areas of learning being tested helps you to decide whether the pupil's answer is satisfactory. **Please note and explain to the class that if all or part of a question has several possible answers, the question number is displayed like this ⑤. If a question has a specific answer, the question number is displayed like this ❺. It is displayed in this way even if the answer is made up of several parts that may be given in any order.**

Some questions test more than one area: for example, a question on writing in the past tense might also check pupils' knowledge of the spelling rules for adding **ed**. In such cases, both parts of the answer must be correct, reflecting real-life situations that require varied knowledge and skills.

Group marking sessions

Some teachers find that group or class marking sessions led by the teacher or classroom assistant are the most effective way of marking the tests: pupils learn by comparing and discussing answers.

Another benefit of group or class marking sessions is that they quickly highlight gaps in pupils' knowledge, which will help to inform your future teaching. Where pupils have given a wrong answer, or none at all, briefly reinforce the key teaching point using an item from this book as a model. At the end of the session, encourage pupils to evaluate their own successes and identify what they need to remember next time or when they are writing.

Suggested questions to ask in a marking session:

- What was this question testing?
- How many different 'correct' answers did we come up with?
- Were some sentence or word choices more interesting or effective than others? Why?
- How do we know this answer is correct?
- How can we make the answer correct?
- Is there an answer that would be even better?
- What are the key points to remember next time?
- When might we put these key points into practice in our reading or writing?

Marking the end-of-section assessments

At the end of each section are two writing assessments: the **Writing task** and the **Proofreading task**. These check that pupils are applying in their writing the knowledge, skills and understanding developed in the weekly tests. The assessments also provide evidence of a pupil's strengths and weaknesses, which will help you to set appropriate targets. You might consider sharing with the pupils a simplified version of the mark scheme – and then involve them in setting their own targets for improving their writing.

The writing task

The **Writing task** helps you assess a pupil's written composition. Prompts help pupils to plan and gather ideas so that when they begin writing they can focus on selecting appropriate grammar, vocabulary and sentence structures to express their ideas clearly and effectively. On pages 16, 30 and 44 you will find photocopiable **Writing task assessment sheets** – one for each section – with specific assessment points arranged under the headings 'Sentence structure and punctuation', 'Composition and effect' and 'Spelling'. Complete one of these sheets as you mark each pupil's work.

The proofreading task

The **Proofreading task** focuses on correcting punctuation, grammar and spelling. Examples of **Completed proofreading tasks** for each section, also photocopiable, are supplied on pages 17, 31 and 45. However, please note that pupils may choose to correct some of the errors using methods different to those shown in the example, but which are equally valid. For example, two main clauses might be joined using a conjunction or separated to make two sentences. Additional evidence gained from the relevant **Proofreading task** will help you to further assess pupils' achievements in 'Sentence punctuation' and 'Spelling' as already assessed in the **Writing task**. If you wish, you can use the photocopiable sheet to make notes on a pupil's work.

Please note: Where the assessment statements reveal weaknesses in a pupil's writing, work with the pupil to identify areas to develop and set targets for future writing. All the books revisit difficult areas so there will also be more opportunities for further practice.

Progress chart

On page 46 of the pupil book you will find a **Progress chart**, with one column each for Sections 1, 2 and 3, and a list of 'I can' statements relating to the kinds of activities practised in the section. Please ask every pupil to complete the relevant column when they have finished working through a section.

The **Progress chart** encourages pupils to monitor their own work by identifying those activities that they have mastered and those requiring further attention. When pupils colour in the chart as recommended (green for easy, orange for getting there and red for difficult), it gives a clear picture of progress. It also shows the benefits of systematic practice: an activity that the pupil cannot perform in Section 1 later gets the 'green light'.

The **Progress chart** promotes self-assessment and personalised learning. However, you may also wish to make a copy for your own record-keeping. For this reason, it may be photocopied.

A Warm-up

Use the word **colour** to write a

① **statement** _Yellow is a bright colour._

② **question** _What is your favourite colour?_

③ **exclamation** _What an amazing colour!_

④ **command** _Colour in the shapes._

⑤ Underline the word that is not a compound noun.

skylark   wagtail   <u>magpie</u>   woodpecker

⑥ Explain your answer.

It is not a compound noun because it
is not made up of two smaller nouns.

⑦ Complete these compound words.

h e a r t broken   g r a p e f r u i t

Add a suffix to make each word into a noun.

⑧ **teach**   _teacher_

⑨ **lonely**   _loneliness_

⑩ **retire**   _retirement_

PART A Focus
1–4: different types of sentence
5–7: compound nouns; words that are often misspelt
8–10: suffixes to form nouns

B Word work

Add the missing letters.

① O l **y** m p i c s   **Clue:** _sporting event_

② s **y** n t h e t i c   **Clue:** _manmade_

③ l **y** r i c s   **Clue:** _the words of a song_

Write a sentence using the word **rose** as a

④ **noun**   _The rose had sharp thorns._

⑤ **verb**   _Smoke rose from the chimney._

⑥ Add the same prefix to complete the words.

auto **matic**   _auto_ **mobile**   _auto_ **pilot**

⑦ What does the prefix mean? _self or by itself_

Write the correct spelling of the underlined words.

⑧ The <u>misterious</u> lights were just an <u>illution</u>.

mysterious   _illusion_

⑨ Their <u>mition</u> was to <u>parashoot</u> in.

mission   _parachute_

⑩ The <u>creacher</u> picked up our <u>sent</u>.

creature   _scent_

PART B Focus
1–3: i sound spelt y
4–5: homonyms; word class
6–7: prefixes to form nouns
8–10: using spelling patterns to correct words

C Sentence work

Add **a** or **an**.

① Joe has _a_ sense of humour.

② It was _an_ expensive mistake.

James seemed _an_ unhappy child.

Cassie and Amy had _an_ argument.

Continue the sentence adding a subordinate clause.

③ The little girl's eyes lit up _as she glimpsed the room full of toys._

④ The boy sat on the bench _while the other children played on the swings._

⑤ The race will begin _when all the contestants are ready._

Underline the adverb in the sentence.

⑥ It was dark <u>outside</u> and an icy wind made me shiver.

⑦ <u>Then</u> they heard a tremendous crash outside the door.

PART C Focus
1–2: using a or an
3–5: developing sentence with subordinate clauses
6–7: identifying adverbs
8–10: writing and punctuating direct speech

Complete the sentences using direct speech.

⑧ The bus driver asked, _"Where do you want to go?"_

⑨ Maria sobbed, _"You have to help me."_

⑩ The security guard shouted, _"Stop right there!"_

X **DEFINITIVE ANSWER**   X **SAMPLE ANSWER**

A Warm-up

1 Underline the three nouns.

The <u>street</u> was full of <u>shoppers</u> with brightly coloured <u>bags</u>.

2 Write three different nouns to change the sentence.

circus   acrobats   costumes

Add a prefix to make a new word.

3 in complete   4 re consider

Add the missing letters.

Clue: types of art

5 s c u l p t u r e

6 a n i m a t i o n

7 i l l u s t r a t i o n

> **PART A Focus**
> 1–2: nouns in sentences
> 3–4: prefixes
> 5–7: words ending ture, ation
> 8–10: words that are often misspelt

The same word is missing from each set of words. Write it in.

8 for wards   for bid   for tune

9 fore cast   fore head   fore ground

10 there fore   be fore   pina fore

B Word work

Write two words that belong to the same word family as the word in **bold**.

1 **fortune** misfortune   unfortunately

2 **cave** cavern   cavity

3 **popular** population   unpopular

Write the meaning of the word in **bold**.

4 He began to **pound** on the door.

pound: hit it hard

5 My heart began to **pound**.

pound: beat fast

6 My stomach **churned**.

churned: turned over

Add the correct prefix to make a word.

mis dis inter

7 **spell** misspell

8 **satisfied** dissatisfied

9 **related** interrelated

> **PART B Focus**
> 1–3: word families
> 4–6: homonyms; inferring meaning from context
> 7–9: rules for adding prefixes
> 10: words ending tion

10 Add the missing letter.

p o s i t i o n   e m o t i o n   p o l l u t i o n

c o m p l e t i o n   t e m p t a t i o n

C Sentence work

1 Use the words **amazed** and **cave** to write a sentence with a main clause and a subordinate clause.

Max was amazed when the wall of the cave opened before his eyes.

Complete the sentence, giving more detail. Add two preposition phrases.

2 He strolled along the quiet lane in the morning sunshine.

3 He hid in the shadows until morning.

4 The girl paddled through the shallow water at the edge of the sea.

> **PART C Focus**
> 1: sentences with more than one clause
> 2–4: using prepositions to show time, place
> 5–7: identifying adjectives and adverbs
> 8–10: checking sentence punctuation

Is the underlined word an adjective or an adverb?

5 He had a <u>wide</u> smile.   adjective

Open your mouth <u>wide</u>.   adverb

6 Everyone has tried <u>hard</u>.   adverb

It is a <u>hard</u> decision.   adjective

7 The clouds are <u>low</u> today.   adjective

Turn the radio down <u>low</u>.   adverb

Add the missing punctuation.

8 "I told you not to come," sighed Matilda. "Why didn't you listen?"

9 He took a deep breath. Then he plunged into the water.

10 Did she really think she could help? How foolish of her! It was too late.

SECTION 1 | Test 3

A Warm-up

Write a two-clause sentence using the words shown.

1 **name before** He wrote his name on the paper before he began to write.

2 **slipped as** She slipped out of the door as it swung slowly open.

3 **swimming although** She kept swimming although the tide was against her.

Write a word beginning with the letters.

4 gui de   bui lding   rui n

5 frui ty   sui t   qui te

Match the word to a suffix to make a new word.

6 agree
7 point
8 tired
9 boast

ness
ment
ful
less

10 Which of the new words are nouns?

agreement   tiredness

PART A Focus
1–3: sentences with subordinate clauses
4–5: tricky spelling patterns
6–9: suffixes
10: word class: nouns

B Word work

Write the correct spelling.

1 encourage   encourage
2 nurishing   nourishing
3 trublesome   troublesome

PART B Focus
1–3: u sound spelt **ou**
4: prefixes to form nouns
5–8: rules for adding suffixes ed, ing
9–10: synonyms

4 Add a prefix to make another noun.

semi circle   mini bus

super nova   sub section

Add the suffixes **ed** and **ing**.

5 **answer**   answered   answering
6 **satisfy**   satisfied   satisfying
7 **quarrel**   quarrelled quarrelling
8 **continue** continued   continuing

Write the words as two sets of synonyms.

**strange ordinary normal
peculiar usual weird**

9 strange   peculiar   weird
10 ordinary   normal   usual

C Sentence work

Continue the sentence by adding another main clause.

1 We have a plan but it might not work.

2 Leo pressed the button and waited for something to happen.

Underline the prepositions in the sentence.

3 On the way, he stopped <u>under</u> the oak tree and took something <u>from</u> his pocket.

4 Since morning, the boat had drifted <u>down</u> the river <u>towards</u> the sea.

PART C Focus
1–2: sentences with two main clauses (using and, but, or)
3–4: identifying prepositions
5–6: using the present perfect tense
7–10: apostrophes in contractions

Rewrite the sentence using the present perfect form of the verb.

5 I forgave him.   I have forgiven him.

6 The king spoke.   The king has spoken.

The plants grew.   The plants have grown.

The pond froze.   The pond has frozen.

Write the contracted form of the underlined words.

7 "I <u>shall not</u> go out if it rains," he explained.   shan't

8 "I told you <u>she would</u> be late," sniffed Angela.   she'd

9 "<u>Do not</u> worry. I <u>will not</u> hurt you," said the gentle giant.   don't   won't

10 Why do contracted forms sound better in sentences like these?

Because they sound more like how someone speaks.

X DEFINITIVE ANSWER   **X** SAMPLE ANSWER

Warm-up

...plete the sentence by adding two preposition ...ses.

They hurried *across the fields towards the village.*

He crouched *in the long grass at the edge of the field.*

They followed the path *through the woods for over an hour.*

...an adverb.

I am ___ *very* ___ late.

He is ___ *often* ___ late.

We are ___ *sometimes* ___ late.

...a word to complete the longer word.

mis *judge* ment

un *grate* ful

dis *appoint* ment

in *effect* ive

PART A Focus
1–3: using prepositions to add detail
4–6: adverbs with adjectives
7–10: word structure: root words, prefixes and suffixes

B Word work

Add the missing syllables.

① en clo *sure*   *Clue: a closed space*

② man *u* fac ture   *Clue: making things*

③ ag ri cul ture   *Clue: farming*

Add **ly** and write the adverb.

④ **extreme**   *extremely*

⑤ **particular**   *particularly*

⑥ **probable**   *probably*

⑦ Write a sentence using two of the adverbs.
It is extremely cold so I probably need a jumper.

Write the meaning of the word in **bold**.

⑧ It was a **dismal** wet morning.
dismal: *gloomy, grey*

⑨ The winners were **elated**.
elated: *very happy*

⑩ Write the plural of the singular noun.

atlas *atlases*   **catalogue** *catalogues*

diary *diaries*   **essay** *essays*

PART B Focus
1–3: words ending ture, sure
4–7: words that are often misspelt; adding ly
8–9: inferring meaning from context
10: forming plurals; rules for adding s/es

Sentence work

There was a strange sound and something happened to the car's engine.

Rewrite the sentence to give a clearer picture of what happened.
There was a hissing sound and smoke began to pour out of the car's engine.

...plete the sentence using one of these subordinating conjunctions.

...e whenever unless

My little brother loved swimming *once he got used to the water.*

Maggie felt nervous *whenever there was a strange sound.*

They decided to stay on the beach *unless it started to rain.*

PART C Focus
1: editing: suggesting improvements
2–4: using a range of subordinating conjunctions
5–7: use of a or an before consonant/vowel sounds
8–10: writing and punctuating direct speech

...a or **an** to complete the sentence.

Bake for *an* hour and *a* half.   ⑦ It is *an* honour to meet *a* hero of mine.

A metre is *a* unit of measurement.

...rite the lines from a script as direct speech.

Merlin: (*looking up*) Is that you, boy?   *"Is that you, boy?" asked Merlin, looking up.*

Boy: (*nervously*) Yes, sir. It is I.   *"Yes, sir. It is I," replied the boy nervously.*

Merlin: Good. Well, come here.   *"Good," said Merlin. "Well, come here."*

X DEFINITIVE ANSWER   **X SAMPLE ANSWER**

A Warm-up

Cross out the second clause and write a different ending for the sentence.

1. She pushed the door open and ~~we all peered inside.~~ light flooded into the room.

2. When Harry finally staggered through the door, ~~he looked exhausted.~~ we were so relieved.

Add the correct word ending.

3. He likes juggle ing .

4. The sky looks menace ing .

5. I was empty ing the bin.

6. Write which of the new words above is

 a noun juggling   **an adjective** menacing

Draw a line to join the prefix to a word to make a new word.

7. inter — natural
8. trans — national
9. anti — atlantic
10. super — social

PART A Focus
1–2: sentences with more than one clause
3–5: adding word endings
6: word classes
7–10: prefixes

B Word work

Write the correct spelling.

1. dissapointed   disappointed

2. iregular   irregular

3. unatural   unnatural

Add the missing letters.

4. The or ches tra tuned up before the ch oir sang.

5. The me chan ic polished the ch rome headlights.

Complete the sentence with a word related to the verb **decide**.

6. We have reached a decision .

7. We were decisive .

Write the meaning of the word in **bold**.

8. He tried to **reclaim** the crown.

 reclaim: get back

9. Water **cascaded** down the sides.

 cascaded: flowed

10. He **extracted** the object from the hole.

 extracted: took out

PART B Focus
1–3: rules for adding prefixes
4–5: k sound spelt ch
6–7: word families and related words
8–10: inferring meaning from context

C Sentence work

1. Why has the writer decided to change the sentence below?

 They warmed their icy hands by the ~~boiling hot~~ fire.

 Because the adjectives are not necessary — we know fire is hot.

Underline the words in the sentence that should start with a capital letter.

2. The <u>scottish</u> explorer <u>david</u> <u>livingstone</u> set out to find the source of the <u>river</u> <u>nile</u>.

3. In <u>august</u> 1875, <u>captain</u> <u>matthew</u> <u>webb</u> swam across the <u>english</u> <u>channel</u>.

4. In <u>britain</u>, the <u>iron</u> <u>age</u> ended when the <u>romans</u> arrived.

Add a subordinate clause that gives a reason **why**. Use a different conjunction each time.

5. Close the door quietly so that the baby does not wake.

6. She pulled on her thickest jumper as it was cold outside.

7. The ship needed a safe port since a storm was coming.

8. He could not see inside the cave because there was no light.

Add two adverbs to complete the sentence.

9. The queen visited here yesterday .

10. When I go to the park, I often see Ben there .

PART C Focus
1: editing: suggesting improvements
2–4: capital letters for proper nouns
5–8: using conjunctions to express cause and reason
9–10: using adverbs to express time and place

X **DEFINITIVE ANSWER**   X **SAMPLE ANSWER**

A Warm-up

Complete the sentence after the conjunction.

1 He did not move while _they climbed down._

2 He did not move because _he was_ _frightened._

3 He did not move although _it was freezing._

4 He did not move until _help arrived._

> **PART A Focus**
> **1–4:** using a range of subordinating conjunctions
> **5–6:** appropriate synonyms
> **7:** words ending **ture**
> **8–10:** suffixes to form nouns

Write three synonyms for the word **thin** in each phrase.

5 a **thin** material   _fine_   _delicate_   _flimsy_

6 a **thin** figure   _slender_   _lean_   _skinny_

7 Add the same ending to complete the words.

struc _ture_   mois _ture_   pos _ture_

Add the same suffix to make the words into nouns.

8 blend _er_   cut _ter_   freeze _er_

9 pave _ment_   apart _ment_   place _ment_

10 bitter _ness_   aware _ness_   shy _ness_

B Word work

Add **ation** to make the verb into a noun.

1 **form**   _formation_

2 **observe**   _observation_

3 **conserve**   _conservation_

4 Use the nouns in these noun phrases.

an _observation_   rock _formation_

wildlife _conservation_

5 Underline the prefix in all these words.

<u>uni</u>t   <u>uni</u>corn   <u>uni</u>form   <u>uni</u>que   <u>uni</u>te

6 What does the prefix mean?   _one_

Write the correct spelling.

7 paticular   _particular_

8 perculiar   _peculiar_

9 nourghty   _naughty_

> **PART B Focus**
> **1–4:** adding ation
> **5–6:** prefixes and word meanings
> **7–9:** words that are often misspelt
> **10:** appropriate synonyms

10 Rewrite the sentence with a synonym in place of **lovely**.

It was a **lovely** view.

It was a spectacular view.

C Sentence work

A nasty, horrible, disgusting smell came from the cave.

1 Write the sentence so that it is more effective.

A sickening smell came from the cave.

Complete the sentence with a list of information.

2 Some of Roald Dahl's most famous books are _Matilda, The BFG and The Twits._

3 To make an electrical circuit, _you will need batteries, wires, a bulb and a switch._

4 In science, we can record our findings _in a table, as a diagram, on a bar chart or on a graph._

Add a prepositional phrase to give a reason.

5 The match was postponed _due to bad weather._

6 Our arms and legs can move _because of our muscles._

Underline the adverb. Explain why it is used.

7 Meet me <u>tomorrow</u> outside the cinema.   _To say when._

8 It was broken and <u>therefore</u> useless.   _To show cause._

9 Dad arrived <u>home</u> on Tuesday.   _To say where._

10 We walked a <u>really</u> long way.   _To give more information._

> **PART C Focus**
> **1:** editing: improving use of adjectives
> **2–4:** using commas to separate items in a list; capital letters
> **5–6:** using prepositions to show cause and effect
> **7–10:** uses of adverbs in sentences

X DEFINITIVE ANSWER   X SAMPLE ANSWER

SECTION 1 | Test 7

A Warm-up

Complete the sentence with three adjectives.

1. The creature's tail was _long, broad and spiky._

2. Its eyes were _round, bulging and bloodshot._

3. Its mouth was _wide, cavernous and drooling._

Add two of these suffixes to the root word to make new words.

ing ment ation

4. **vary** _varying_ _variation_

5. **manage** _managing_ _management_

6. **separate** _separating_ _separation_

Add a preposition to complete each phrase.

7. _against_ the clock

8. _around_ the world

9. _beyond_ the rainbow

10. _beside_ the sea

> **PART A Focus**
> **1–3:** adjectives for effect; use of commas
> **4–6:** rules for adding suffixes
> **7–10:** prepositions

B Word work

Write a word related to the word in **bold**.

1. **school** _scholar_

2. **chemist** _chemical_

3. **technical** _technology_

> **PART B Focus**
> **1–3:** word families; spelling patterns
> **4–6:** rules for adding prefixes and suffixes
> **7:** homonyms; word classes
> **8–10:** nouns with prefixes

Complete the word sum.

4. **un + earth + ed** = _unearthed_

5. **dis + solve + ing** = _dissolving_

6. **im + possible + ly** = _impossibly_

7. Write a sentence to show how the word **last** can be used as an

   adjective _I had the last cake._

   adverb _He arrived last._

8. Add the prefix **mega** to make three words.

   mega **star** _mega_ **store** _mega_ **phone**

9. What does the prefix **mega** mean?

   very large

10. What would a megacity be?

    a very large city

C Sentence work

1. Continue the sentence with a subordinate clause.

   He crept closer _until he could hear the two men talking._

2. Continue the sentence with a main clause.

   He crept closer _but he still could not see into the room._

Rewrite the sentence using the present perfect form of the verb to show that events are still happening.

3. **I thought about this for a while.** _I have thought about this for a while._

4. **He went to watch the match.** _He has gone to watch the match._

5. **We now reached the top.** _We have now reached the top._

Proofread and correct the punctuation.

6. How could Greta help them.? ^S she was only ten years old.

7. He asked when ^S stonehenge was built. ^W what a brilliant question.!

8. "You'll need gloves, scarves and boots," said Oliver. "Don't forget."

> **PART C Focus**
> **1–2:** sentences with more than one clause
> **3–5:** using the present perfect form
> **6–8:** proofreading to check for punctuation errors
> **9–10:** using a range of conjunctions

Finish the sentence after the conjunction.

9. **The old clock won't work unless** _you wind it every day._

10. **He stepped out of the door just as** _Josephine turned the corner._

X DEFINITIVE ANSWER   X SAMPLE ANSWER

A Warm-up

Write a more precise noun phrase to replace the one underlined.

1. The wizard put <u>some stuff</u> into the cauldron.
   a sprinkle of magic powder

2. They ate <u>a bit of food</u>.
   a few crusts of stale bread

3. I have just finished <u>a book</u>.
   a fascinating story about a refugee

Write a word that fits in both phrases.

4. a b *ow* and arrow   take a b *ow*

5. a birthday p *resent*   the p *resent* tense

6. a dog's l *ead*   a pencil l *ead*

Underline the word that is not a synonym.

7. tangy sour <u>smooth</u> sharp

8. quiver quake <u>quaint</u> tremble

9. wriggle writhe squirm <u>saunter</u>

10. puzzled <u>proved</u> perplexed mystified

> **PART A Focus**
> **1–3:** editing: using more precise noun phrases
> **4–6:** homonyms and homographs
> **7–10:** identifying synonyms

B Word work

Write the correct spelling of the noun phrase.

1. Sicamore Cresent   *Sycamore Crescent*
2. a dangerus asent   *a dangerous ascent*
3. a fasinating subjekt   *a fascinating subject*

Use the correct word in each sentence.

business busyness

4. He works in the music *business* .
5. Joe liked the *busyness* of the classroom.

Write the plural of the noun.

6. **grass** *grasses*   **moss** *mosses*
7. **bamboo** *bamboos*   **cactus** *cactuses/cacti*

Write the meaning of the word in **bold**.

8. I tried to **retrieve** the ball.
   retrieve: *get it back*

9. The game will **resume** shortly.
   resume: *start again*

10. They tried to **repel** the enemy.
    repel: *push back*

> **PART B Focus**
> **1–3:** spelling patterns: sc, y, ou
> **4–5:** words that are often confused
> **6–7:** plurals and plural spellings
> **8–10:** inferring meaning from context

C Sentence work

Is the underlined word a conjunction or a preposition?

1. We went for pizza <u>after</u> the match.   preposition
2. We checked the time <u>before</u> we left.   conjunction
3. We will not be home <u>until</u> 6 o'clock.   preposition
4. They have been celebrating <u>since</u> they won the lottery.   conjunction

> **PART C Focus**
> **1–4:** identifying conjunctions and prepositions
> **5–7:** punctuating direct speech with inverted commas and other punctuation
> **8–9:** adverbs to show time and place
> **10:** using conjunctions, adverbs and prepositions to add detail

Add the missing punctuation.

5. "This can't be the right place," said Aunt Sally. "Let's look at the invitation again."

6. "We must leave," sighed his mother, "because the soldiers are coming."

7. "Well," said Chloe, "it all started when I left my bag at the checkout."

8. Complete the sentences with an adverb to say **where**.

   He flung the key *outside* .   She took a step *closer* .

9. Complete the sentence with an adverb to say **when**.

   We spoke *afterwards* .   Come and visit me *soon* .

10. Rewrite the sentence giving more detail. Use a conjunction, adverb and preposition.

   People stopped and stared.

   Suddenly, people stopped and stared as they saw the car rolling down the hill.

X **DEFINITIVE ANSWER** X **SAMPLE ANSWER**

A Warm-up

Complete the sentence with a preposition phrase to explain.

1. **when** He scurried off *at midnight.*
2. **where** He scurried off *into his workshop.*
3. **how** He scurried off *in a hurry.*
4. **why** He scurried off *because of the rain.*

Write a sentence using the adverb formed from the adjective.

5. He was nimble.

   He leapt nimbly over the fence.

6. It was accidental.

   I did it accidentally.

7. It was a dismal failure.

   We failed dismally.

Write a word belonging to the same word family.

8. **voice** *vocal*
9. **royal** *royalty*
10. **chorus** *choral*

PART A Focus
1–4: using prepositions to add detail
5–7: adding **ly** to form adverbs; using adverbs
8–10: word families

B Word work

Draw a line to match the sentence to the word class of the word **warm**.

1. It is a very warm day. — verb
2. Warm the milk in the pan. — noun
3. Have a warm by the fire. — adjective

Write a sentence using the word **lean** as

4. **an adjective** *He was tall and lean.*
5. **a verb** *Lean against the wall.*

6. Underline the plural noun that is incorrect.

   volcanoes   potatoes   <u>pianoes</u>   echoes

Add a prefix to make an adjective that means the opposite.

7. **mature** *immature*
8. **responsible** *irresponsible*
9. **regular** *irregular*

PART B Focus
1–5: word classes
6: plural spellings
7–9: adding prefixes **im ir**
10: words ending **sion**

10. Add the same ending to spell three nouns.

    ero *sion*   ver *sion*   vi *sion*

C Sentence work

Is the underlined word a conjunction or an adverb?

1. We can go outside <u>once</u> the rain stops.   conjunction
2. I have only been to Spain <u>once</u>.   adverb

PART C Focus
1–2: identifying conjunctions and adverbs
3–5: writing sentences with more than one clause
6–8: editing: suggesting improvements
9–10: use of a/an

Write a complete sentence with a main and subordinate clause.

3. **Everything** *was peaceful in the village before they built the new road.*
4. **An eagle** *was hovering overhead as the boy stood on the cliff top.*
5. **Food** *is chewed before swallowing so that it breaks down.*

Edit the sentence so it uses the fewest possible words. Cross out the extra words. Check the punctuation.

6. ~~Then just at that moment~~ A ~~a loud~~ dog barked. ~~noisily somewhere.~~
7. ~~So~~ Oliver ~~just~~ ran. ~~away as fast as he could.~~
8. ~~It seemed like~~ M ~~many~~ hours passed. ~~with nothing happening.~~

9. Why is the word **an** used in this sentence rather than **a**? **He was an honest man.**

   Because you can't hear the 'h' at the start of 'honest'. It starts with a vowel sound.

10. Why is the word **a** used in this sentence? **He wore a uniform.**

    Because the letter 'u' at the start of 'uniform' makes a consonant sound ('y').

X DEFINITIVE ANSWER   X SAMPLE ANSWER

A Warm-up

Add a subordinate clause.

(1) The last customers were leaving *when we arrived at the shop.*

(2) The lights were shining brightly *as it was already getting dark.*

Complete the sentence using the word **an** twice.

(3) For lunch, I had *an apple and an ice cream.*

(4) In the wood, I saw *an owl in an oak tree.*

Draw a line to match the synonyms.

(5) replied — enquired
(6) protested — responded
(7) asked — commanded
(8) ordered — objected

(5) replied → responded; (6) protested → objected; (7) asked → enquired; (8) ordered → commanded)

> **PART A Focus**
> **1–2:** sentences with more than one clause
> **3–4:** use of a/an
> **5–8:** synonyms
> **9–10:** tion spelling; adjective suffixes

Write the adjective to match the definition.

(9) fun *ctional*   works well
(10) mo *tionless*   not moving

B Word work

Write two synonyms for the word **terrible** in each phrase.

(1) a **terrible** noise   *horrific*   *frightening*
(2) a **terrible** smell   *revolting*   *unpleasant*
(3) a **terrible** mistake   *awful*   *dreadful*

Write the correct spelling of the underlined words.

(4) I did not concider it a consern.
  consider   *concern*

(5) The insident was an axsident.
  incident   *accident*

(6) Let me concult the kalender.
  consult   *calendar*

> **PART B Focus**
> **1–3:** appropriate synonyms
> **4–6:** words that are often misspelt (c and s spellings)
> **7–8:** prefixes and word meanings
> **9–10:** sh sound spelt ch

Underline the word that does not share the same prefix.

(7) **bicycle   binoculars   billion   biplane**

(8) How do you know?   *It does not have a meaning linked to 'two'.*

Add the missing letters. **ch sh**

(9) fa **sh** ion   bro **ch** ure   qui **ch** e

(10) sa **ch** et   cu **sh** ion   ma **ch** ine

C Sentence work

Complete the sentence to show cause and effect. Use the adverb **therefore** in the sentence.

> **PART C Focus**
> **1–3:** using adverb **therefore** to show cause and effect
> **4–6:** prepositions to show time, place and direction
> **7–10:** use of apostrophe in place of missing letters

(1) It was snowing and *therefore school was closed on Monday.*

(2) The farmer's crops had failed and *therefore his family were hungry.*

(3) The bag is made from a lightweight material and *therefore easy to carry.*

Sort the preposition phrases that show time, place and direction.

down the street, at midnight, to the cinema, during assembly, at school, between the gates, on Tuesday, after tea, in the shop, on top of the hill, over the fence, towards the hall

(4) **time** *at midnight, during assembly, on Tuesday, after tea*

(5) **place** *at school, between the gates, in the shop, on top of the hill*

(6) **direction** *down the street, to the cinema, over the fence, towards the hall*

Write the sentence using an apostrophe correctly.

(7) "I told em not to come," she said.   *"I told 'em not to come," she said.*

(8) I was just thinking bout the party.   *I was just thinking 'bout the party.*

(9) "Ere, what's all this, then?" he said.   *"'Ere, what's all this, then?" he said.*

(10) Why is an apostrophe needed?   *To show that there is a missing letter.*

 DEFINITIVE ANSWER    SAMPLE ANSWER

A Warm-up

Complete the sentence to give a reason.

1 He rolled over so that *he could get a better view.*

2 Spiders build webs in order to *catch food.*

3 The Post Office was closed as *it was Sunday.*

Write two synonyms for the word **bad** in each phrase.

4 **bad** news — *unpleasant*   *unwelcome*

5 a **bad** accident — *serious*   *severe*

6 **bad** behaviour — *naughty*   *unruly*

7 Write four words that belong to the same word family as the word **vision**.

visible   *television*   *invisible*   *visor*

Add the missing letter.

8 s c **i** n t i l l a t i n g

9 h **y** s t e r i c a l

10 c h **a** m e l e o n

> **PART A Focus**
> **1–3:** conjunctions to give reasons
> **4–6:** appropriate synonyms
> **7:** word families
> **8–10:** spelling patterns

B Word work

Add a suffix to the word to make an adjective.

1 **fret** *fretful*   **3** **fancy** *fanciful*

2 **flaw** *flawless*   **4** **fury** *furious*

Add the suffix **ly** to make the word into an adverb.

5 **dismal** *dismally*   **6** **visible** *visibly*

Underline the words that are wrongly spelt. Write the correct spellings.

7 He had no <u>expeareance</u> of <u>bizness</u>.

experience   *business*

8 I have <u>recoverd</u> from my <u>resent</u> <u>acsident</u>.

recovered   *recent*   *accident*

9 He <u>mist</u> on three <u>seprate</u> <u>ocassions</u>.

missed   *separate*   *occasions*

> **PART B Focus**
> **1–4:** adjective suffixes; rules for adding suffixes
> **5–6:** rules for adding **ly**
> **7–9:** words that are often misspelt
> **10:** singular and plural nouns

10 Write the singular form of the noun.

people *person*   **dormice** *dormouse*

dominoes *domino*   **sheep** *sheep*

C Sentence work

1 Complete the sentence with a list of noun phrases.

The princess opened her presents and found *a silver comb, a pair of golden slippers, a dress of silky feathers and a diamond tiara.*

2 Complete the sentence with a list of actions.

In his anger, *he slammed the door, ran upstairs, threw himself on the bed and began to cry.*

Continue the sentence to explain more about paragraphs.

3 A paragraph is a group of sentences *within a piece of writing.*

4 You start a new line *at the beginning of a new paragraph.*

5 Paragraphs are important *because they help to break up our writing.*

Complete the sentence using the present perfect form of the verb in **bold**.

6 **plan** We *have planned* a surprise party for tomorrow.

7 **choose** We *have chosen* the decorations.

8 **write** We *have written* the invitations.

9 **hide** We *have hidden* the presents.

10 Why has the perfect form been used? *Because the events are still ongoing.*

> **PART C Focus**
> **1–2:** using commas in a list; noun phrases and actions
> **3–5:** using prepositions and conjunctions to develop ideas; use of paragraphs
> **6–10:** present perfect form rather than simple past tense

X DEFINITIVE ANSWER   X SAMPLE ANSWER

A Warm-up

Write a two-clause sentence using the given verbs.

1. **swerved scattered** The bus swerved onto the pavement and people scattered.

2. **scrambled disappeared** He scrambled to his feet as the robbers disappeared from view.

Underline the word that is not a synonym.

3. reclaim recover <u>reduce</u> regain

4. <u>endless</u> pointless useless worthless

Write a sentence using the word in **bold** as a noun and a verb.

PART A Focus
1–2: sentences with more than one clause
3–4: synonyms; word structure
5–6: homonyms; word class
7–10: tricky spellings

5. **spring** In spring, lambs spring about the fields.

6. **park** Let's park the car by the park.

Add the missing letter.

7. i m a **g** i n e

8. f r a **g** i l e

9. m a r **g** i n

10. v e **g** e t a b l e

B Word work

Write the correct spelling.

1. shampaine   champagne

2. chandeleer   chandelier

3. sharardes   charades

PART B Focus
1–3: sh sound spelt ch
4–6: rules for adding **ation**
7: synonyms in context
8–10: word families

Add **ation** to make the verb into a noun.

4. separate ion

5. vary iation

6. experiment ation

7. Write a synonym for **bad**.

   a **bad** day unpleasant   a **bad** person evil

Why do these words belong to the same word family?

structure construct destruction

Give two reasons.

8. They all contain the same root 'struct'.

9. They all mean something to do with building.

10. Write another word belonging to this word family.   construction

C Sentence work

1. Proofread the sentences. Add the missing punctuation.

   Mrs Bagshaw said she was concerned about the town's new supermarket. "What about my shop?" she asked reporters. "We rely on local people shopping here."

Underline the adverb in the sentence. Write a sentence using the same word as a preposition.

2. Rats were scurrying <u>about</u>.   The journey took about an hour.

3. The shelves fell <u>down</u>.   The car rolled down the hill.

4. White clouds floated <u>above</u>.   The plane flew above the clouds.

Complete the sentence after the conjunction.

5. I like to take things easy whereas my family like to be active.

6. I will never learn to juggle even if I practise every day.

7. Dad always goes jogging whether it is hot or cold.

Cross out any words that you think are unnecessary.

PART C Focus
1: proofreading: checking punctuation
2–4: identifying adverbs; using prepositions
5–7: using a range of conjunctions
8–10: editing: suggesting improvements

8. A flashing light beamed from the ~~glass~~ window of the ~~tall~~ tower ~~building~~.

9. ~~The reason why~~ he was angry ~~was~~ because someone had lied.

10. Marble is a ~~sort of very~~ hard ~~type of~~ stone with ~~all sorts of~~ coloured patterns ~~in it~~.

Remind the pupil to complete Section 1 of the Progress chart on page 46 of the pupil book.

X **DEFINITIVE ANSWER**   X **SAMPLE ANSWER**

Writing task assessment sheet: The children's garden

Name: _____ Class/Set: _____

Teacher's name: _____ Date: _____

Sentence structure and punctuation

	Always/often	Sometimes	Never
Sentences with more than one clause are used			
A range of conjunctions is used			
Adverbs, prepositions and conjunctions are used to add detail about time, place and cause			
Expanded noun phrases with carefully chosen adjectives are used			
A variety of sentence types is used			
Appropriate use of tense, including use of present perfect forms			
Sentences are demarcated accurately with full stops, capital letters, ? or !			
Commas are used in lists of words or phrases			
Apostrophes are used for contractions and possession			

Composition and effect

Features of leaflet form are used (e.g. sense of purpose to inform and persuade)			
Simple organisational features are used (e.g. subheadings)			
Ideas are developed in paragraphs around themes			
Connections are made between ideas			
Careful choices of vocabulary are made			
Appropriate tone is used (e.g. friendly)			

Spelling

Knowledge of spelling patterns is applied correctly			
Longer words are correct, including suffixes and endings			
Correct spelling of words that are often misspelt			
Words with prefixes are correct			
Rules for adding verb endings and suffixes are applied correctly			
Spelling of plurals is correct			
Common homophones are correct			

Writing task summary

ompleted proofreading task: Thank you letter

ame: _____ Class/Set: _____

acher's name: _____ Date: _____

ear Michael,

iank you for coming to talk to us about the p*y*ramids in ~~egipt~~ *E**y*. and for
isering all our questions. ~~y~~*Y*ou know an awful~~l~~ lot about the subject.
 w

  c
was fas~~s~~inating to hear about your exper*i*ences*.*. ~~y~~*Y*ou were so lucky to
~~tchelly~~ *tually* see the ~~tresheres~~ *treasures* inside the b*u*ildings. You di~~s~~*c*ribed it so well.
id the photogra~~ffs~~*ph* and illustra~~shuns~~*tio*ns helped us to rea~~l~~*l*y ima~~j~~*g*ine what it
is like.

ive you been on any more digs lat~~l~~*el*ey? ~~i~~*I*t must be so int*e*resting to visit
her countr~~y~~*ie*s and discov*e*r all about people*'*s li~~f~~*v*es.

  ture
ease come and tell us about your next adven~~cher~~.

ur's sincere~~le~~y,

arlie Bagshaw

oofreading task summary

ction 1 tasks summary

A Warm-up

Complete the sentence to say

1. **when** The genie appeared in the morning.

2. **where** The genie appeared in the ballroom.

3. **how** The genie appeared in a puff of smoke.

4. Add the same ending to make three words with similar meanings.

   frant ic   hect ic   chaot ic

Complete the sentence using a noun formed from the word in **bold**.

5. **determined** He has great determination.

6. **inspired** I had sudden inspiration.

7. **observes** He made his observations.

Write the root word.

8. **carriage** carry

9. **barrier** bar

10. **citizen** city

PART A Focus
1–3: prepositions to add detail
4: words ending ic
5–7: adding ation
8–10: root words

B Word work

Add the missing letters.

1. d i a l o g u e   *Clue: a conversation*

2. c a t a l o g u e   *Clue: a list of items*

3. i n t r i g u i n g   *Clue: fascinating*

Add the same suffix to make adjectives. **ic al ive**

4. hero ic   magnet ic   idiot ic

5. music al   centre al   approve al

6. decorate ive attract ive   invent ive

Write the correct spelling.

7. threatning   threatening

   deafning   deafening

Write the meaning of the word in **bold**.

8. I **intervened** to stop them fighting.

   intervened: came between them

9. It was **extraordinary**.

   extraordinary: very unusual

10. He found **microscopic** creatures.

    microscopic: only visible under a microscope

PART B Focus
1–3: spelling patterns: gue
4–6: suffixes to form adjectives
7: spelling errors; adding suffixes
8–10: inferring meaning from word structure

C Sentence work

Rewrite the sentence so that it starts with the conjunction. Punctuate the sentence correctly.

1. The tide was strong although the water was not deep.

   Although the water was not deep, the tide was strong.

2. The jaws of the plant clamp shut once an insect lands.

   Once an insect lands, the jaws of the plant clamp shut.

3. All will be lost unless help arrives soon. Unless help arrives soon, all will be lost.

Underline the longest noun phrase in the sentence below.

4. Pass me <u>the striped beach towel from the bag on the chair</u>.

5. Why have words and phrases been added to the noun? To say exactly which towel.

Add words and phrases to the noun to write a longer noun phrase.

6. **programme**   the fascinating television programme about bees

7. **tree**   the ancient oak tree in the middle of the park

Underline the determiners in the sentence.

8. <u>Two</u> players were tied in <u>first</u> place.

9. There were <u>no</u> goals in <u>the</u> match.

10. <u>Both</u> teams missed <u>several</u> attempts.

PART C Focus
1–3: fronted subordinate clauses; commas after fronted adverbials
4–7: expanded noun phrases to specify nouns
8–10: identifying determiners

ⓧ DEFINITIVE ANSWER   ⓧ SAMPLE ANSWER

A Warm-up

Underline the preposition. Write a different preposition to replace it.

1 We sat <u>beneath</u> the trees. under

2 Amy finished right <u>behind</u> us. after

3 He shouted <u>above</u> the noise. over

4 I spotted Joe <u>among</u> the crowd. in

Add the prefix and suffix.

5 im possible ly

6 il legal ly

7 in correct ly

> **PART A Focus**
> **1–4:** prepositions to show place
> **5–7:** rules for adding prefixes and suffixes
> **8–9:** homonyms; word classes
> **10:** spelling patterns

Write a sentence using the word **form** as a

8 **noun** Fill in the form.

9 **verb** Ice can form on ponds.

Add the missing letters to these foods.

10 q u i c h e   m e r i n g u e
    b i s c u i t s

B Word work

Write the phrase correctly.

1 beach trees   beech trees

2 hills and veils   hills and vales

3 the king's rain   the king's reign

Add the correct suffix to make a noun.

ive ist ant

4 cycle ist   motor ist   novel ist

5 detect ive   relate ive

6 serve ant   contest ant

> **PART B Focus**
> **1–3:** homophones
> **4–6:** suffixes to form nouns; rules for adding suffixes
> **7:** words ending ic
> **8–10:** choosing appropriate synonyms

Write the correct spelling.

7 drastik drastic   frantick frantic

Write two synonyms for the word **dull**.

8 a **dull** day   overcast   sunless

9 a **dull** thud   muffled   indistinct

10 a **dull** book   unexciting   boring

C Sentence work

Twigs touched his face like gnarled fingers.

1 Why has the writer used this simile?   To create a frightening effect.

Complete these similes to create a similar mood. Add an interesting noun phrase.

2 The sound of thunder was like a growling monster in the sky.

3 The sea was like a boiling cauldron.

4 The cold wind was like icy knives through the winter air.

Underline the pronoun in the sentence.

5 Most rocks are hidden under a layer of soil but <u>some</u> are exposed on cliffs and mountains.

6 I had collected many shells before but <u>these</u> were different.

7 We were looking for fossils but we could not find <u>any</u>.

> **PART C Focus**
> **1–4:** constructing similes using like and a noun phrase
> **5–7:** identifying pronouns
> **8–10:** apostrophe for plural possession; correcting misuse of apostrophes with plural s

Write the sentence correctly.

8 The babies parent's were delighted.   The babies' parents were delighted.

9 The fishermens boat's were empty.   The fishermen's boats were empty.

10 The dragons tails' beat furiously.   The dragons' tails beat furiously.

X DEFINITIVE ANSWER   X SAMPLE ANSWER

A Warm-up

Complete the sentence after the conjunction.

1. Switch off the lights whenever _you leave the room._

2. The dog followed him wherever _he went._

3. Marie likes toast whereas _I prefer porridge._

> **PART A Focus**
> **1–3:** using a range of conjunctions
> **4–6:** appropriate synonyms
> **7–10:** words ending ous

Write two synonyms for the word **hot** in each phrase.

4. **hot** food   _spicy_   _fiery_

5. **hot** temper   _fierce_   _angry_

6. **hot** weather   _sweltering_   _scorching_

Add the same suffix to make three words with similar meanings.

7. peril _ous_   9. treacher _ous_

8. hazard _ous_

10. Write a sentence using two of the words.

It was a hazardous journey along treacherous roads.

B Word work

Add **ation**. Check the spelling of the noun.

1. **transform**   _transformation_

2. **exclaim**   _exclamation_

3. **combine**   _combination_

4. **pollen**   _pollination_

5. Add the same prefix to these words. The prefix means **not**.

im possible   im patient

im mature   im mobile

> **PART B Focus**
> **1–4:** adding **ation**; exceptions to rule
> **5:** adding prefixes: im
> **6–7:** spelling patterns
> **8–10:** shades of meaning in synonyms

Add the missing letters.

6. intrig _u_ e   g _u_ e st   vag _u_ e ly

7. disg _u_ i se   peng _u_ i n   disting _u_ i sh

Write two words that mean

8. **very happy**   _ecstatic_   _elated_

9. **very angry**   _furious_   _irate_

10. **very careful** _cautious_   _wary_

C Sentence work

Rewrite the sentence so that it starts with the adverbial.

1. He was in a different room when he woke up.

When he woke up, he was in a different room.

2. Everyone had disappeared much to his amazement.

Much to his amazement, everyone had disappeared.

3. New skin is replacing old skin all the time.

All the time, new skin is replacing old skin.

Complete the sentence and add the punctuation.

4. "Wait   here," said   Mr   Granville, "until _your teacher arrives."_

5. "I   have   the   key," said   Maxine, "so _we can let ourselves in."_

6. "You   must   put   your   boots   on," said   the   farmer, "because _the fields are very muddy."_

7. "Will   you   go   to   the   farm   shop," said   Mum, "and _get me some eggs?"_

Underline the word that is not Standard English. Write it correctly.

> **PART C Focus**
> **1–3:** identifying and fronting adverbials; commas after fronted adverbials
> **4–7:** punctuating split direct speech with inverted commas and other punctuation
> **8–10:** Standard English verb forms and agreement

8. United have <u>beat</u> City one-nil.   _beaten_

9. United <u>was</u> lucky to win.   _were_

10. The other teams have <u>drawed</u>.   _drawn_

X **DEFINITIVE ANSWER**   X **SAMPLE ANSWER**

A Warm-up

Continue the sentence by adding another clause.
Use a co-ordinating conjunction.

1 The man spoke *and everyone listened*
   to him.

2 She warned them *but they did not*
   listen.

3 We must water the plants *or they*
   will die.

Write a verb to describe how the animal moved.

4 The elephants were *lumbering.*

5 The horses were *galloping.*

6 Crabs were *scuttling* about.

Draw a line to join the prefix to a word so it makes a new word.

7 sub   navigate
8 circum   change
9 super   section
10 inter   sonic

> **PART A Focus**
> **1–3:** sentences with more than one clause; co-ordinating conjunctions
> **4–6:** verb choice; adding **ing**
> **7–10:** prefixes

B Word work

Add the missing letters.

1 p l a **q u e**   *Clue: forms on teeth*
2 o p **a** q u e   *Clue: not clear*
3 t e **c** h **n** i q u e   *Clue: method*
4 p i c **t u r** e s **q u** e *Clue: pretty, attractive*

Complete the noun phrase with an adjective formed from the word in **bold**.

5 **drama**   a *dramatic*   ending
6 **mystery** a *mysterious* stranger
7 **fact**   a *factual*   account

Write the meaning of the word in **bold**.

8 Metals **contract**.   *shrink*
9 He signed a **contract**.   *an agreement*

10 Add the correct word.

accept except

He will *accept* the job.

He told everyone *except* me.

> **PART B Focus**
> **1–4:** spelling patterns
> **5–7:** suffixes to form adjectives; rules for adding suffixes
> **8–9:** homonyms/homographs; inferring meaning from context
> **10:** near homophones

C Sentence work

1 Change the mood in the sentence. Cross out words and write new ones.

~~White, fluffy~~ clouds ~~floated gently~~ above. *dark, sinister   hung heavily*

Add a noun, adjective and preposition phrase to expand and specify the noun.

2 **shop**   *the delightful cake shop on the corner of Hurst Street*
3 **inspector** *the new police inspector in charge of the case*
4 **present**   *the brilliant birthday present from my grandad*

> **PART C Focus**
> **1:** editing: suggesting changes to vocabulary
> **2–4:** noun phrases with modifying adjectives, nouns and preposition phrases
> **5–7:** expressive language; using conjunctions
> **8–10:** commas after fronted adverbials

Complete the sentence after the conjunction.

5 The pot began to bubble as if *it might explode.*

6 He began to laugh as if *someone was tickling him with a feather.*

7 The teacher looked at him as if *he might be mad.*

Add the missing commas.

8 Far, far away, there was a city that stood beside the sea.

9 In the north of the country, on the edge of a dark forest, there was a small stone cottage.

10 All of a sudden, with an almighty roar, the monster awoke.

A Warm-up

Complete the sentence by adding two preposition phrases.

1 They hurried _across the fields towards the village._

2 He crouched _in the long grass for nearly an hour._

Write the correct spelling.

3 ordinry _ordinary_

4 moden _modern_

Underline the word that is not a homophone.

5 saw sore soar <u>sour</u>

6 paw pour poor <u>peer</u>

7 their there <u>they</u> they're

PART A Focus
1–2: using prepositions to add detail
3–4: words that are often misspelt
5–7: homophones
8–10: tricky words; adding ly

Write the adverb that means

8 **very** e x t r <u>e</u> m e <u>l</u> y

9 **not together** s e p <u>a</u> r a t e <u>l</u> y

10 **most likely** p r o b <u>a</u> b l y

B Word work

Add the missing letter. **i e**

1 o b v <u>i</u> o u s   c u r <u>i</u> o u s
   p r e v <u>i</u> o u s

2 h i d <u>e</u> o u s   c o u r t <u>e</u> o u s
   g o r g <u>e</u> o u s

Complete the sentence with an adverb formed from the word in **bold**.

3 A **hero** behaves _heroically_ .

4 The **frantic** man waved _frantically_ .

Write the root word of the word in **bold**.

PART B Focus
1–2: words ending **ious**, **eous**
3–4: adding ly; exceptions
5–10: inferring word meaning from word structure

5 highly **flammable** _flame_

6 a **futuristic** car _future_

7 his **memoirs** _memory_

Write the meaning of the word in **bold**.

8 **flammable** _easy to catch fire_

9 **futuristic** _ahead of time_

10 **memoirs** _a book of memories or about a life_

C Sentence work

Underline the adverbials in the sentence below.

1 We <u>finally</u> found the tickets <u>after many hours of searching</u>.

PART C Focus
1–3: identifying and fronting adverbials; commas after fronted adverbials
4–6: apostrophe for singular possession
7: word classes: adverbs, adjectives
8–10: using a range of determiners

Rewrite the sentence twice, each time beginning with one of the adverbials.

2 _After many hours of searching, we finally found the tickets._

3 _Finally, we found the tickets after many hours of searching._

Underline the word or words that need a possessive apostrophe. Write them correctly.

4 St <u>Pauls</u> Cathedral is one of <u>Londons</u> most famous buildings.   _St Paul's_   _London's_

5 It was the youngest <u>princesses</u> birthday.   _princess's_

6 <u>Jameses</u> head was stuck in the <u>schools</u> railings.   _James's_   _school's_

Write a sentence using the word **fast** as an

7 **adverb** _Cheetahs run fast._   **adjective** _This is a fast car._

Add determiners to complete the sentence. Do not use **the** or **a**.

8 At _her_ party, there was _enough_ food for _thirty_ people.

9 After _several_ weeks of rain, _many_ people were hoping for _some_ sunshine.

10 _All_ pupils should wear _their_ uniforms to school _every_ day.

X DEFINITIVE ANSWER   X SAMPLE ANSWER

A Warm-up

Complete the noun phrase with a suitable adjective.

1. an __endangered__ animal
2. an __adventurous__ life
3. an __unfortunate__ accident

> **PART A Focus**
> **1–3:** use of a or an; adjectives in noun phrases
> **4:** word families
> **5–7:** prepositions
> **8–10:** words ending ous

4. Why do these words not belong to the same word family?

   gravel gravity gravy

   __Because they do not have the same__
   __root word.__

Add a preposition to complete the sentence.

5. I spotted him hiding __among__ the trees.
6. Try not to eat sweets __between__ meals.
7. The book was __about__ recycling.

Add the missing letters

8. t r e m e n d o u s   *Clue: wonderful*
9. l u m i n o u s   *Clue: shines brightly*
10. h i l a r i o u s   *Clue: very funny*

B Word work

Underline the word that is wrong. Write it correctly.

1. Did the knight <u>sleigh</u> a dragon?   slay
2. Blood flows through your <u>vains</u>.   veins
3. The lion hunted its <u>pray</u>.   prey
4. He wanted to <u>conker</u> the world.   conquer

Write words formed from the verb.

verb	noun	adjective	adverb
5. **act**	activity	active	actively
6. **create**	creation	creative	creatively

Write a word that means

7. **a little alike**   similar
8. **very alike**   identical

> **PART B Focus**
> **1–4:** homophones
> **5–6:** using suffixes to change word class
> **7–8:** shades of meaning in synonyms
> **9–10:** adding prefixes

Add a prefix to make a word meaning the opposite of the word in **bold**.

9. Jake is very **responsible**.   irresponsible
10. Beth's writing is **legible**.   illegible

C Sentence work

1. Edit, extend and improve this sentence.

   There was serpents moving in the dark.

   __On the floor of the chamber, there were hundreds of serpents slithering about in the darkness.__

Write a sentence of direct speech including the word in **bold**.

2. "Come on,"   **moaned** Joe, "or we will be late."
3. "We could go to the park,"   **suggested** Dad, "if it stops raining."
4. "Bring it here,"   **demanded** the head teacher, "and stop wasting time."
5. "Look out!"   **shrieked** Beth. "That car's coming fast."

Complete the sentence. Use a pronoun in place of the underlined noun or noun phrase.

6. Many <u>trees</u> lose their leaves in autumn but __some stay green all year.__
7. Do you prefer savoury <u>foods</u> or __sweet ones?__
8. He tried reading <u>the other book</u> but __that was too difficult for him.__

Underline the word that is not Standard English. Write it correctly.

9. It <u>don't</u> matter what you say.   doesn't
10. Ben and Max <u>was</u> jogging to the finish.   were

> **PART C Focus**
> **1:** editing: checking grammar and suggesting improvements
> **2–5:** writing and punctuating split direct speech
> **6–8:** accurate use of pronouns to avoid repetition
> **9–10:** Standard English verb forms and agreement

X DEFINITIVE ANSWER   X SAMPLE ANSWER

A Warm-up

Underline the adverb. Write a different adverb to replace it.

1. The train arrives <u>soon</u> at platform ten. *later*

2. He <u>always</u> parks his car by the gate. *often*

3. I finished my new book <u>yesterday</u>. *today*

4. Add the missing letters to make three words that mean jumpy or edgy.

   nerv *ous*   anxi *ous*   rest *less*

5. Write a sentence using two of the words.

   Everyone was feeling anxious and I was
   really nervous about the result.

Add the missing ending.

6. a mountain *ous* place

7. a cavern *ous* place

> **PART A Focus**
> **1–3:** adverbs to express time
> **4–7:** adjectives; ous, less
> **8–10:** spelling

Add the missing letters.

Clue: *places of worship*

8. s y n a g o g u e

9. c a t h e d r a l

10. m o s q u e

B Word work

Is the underlined word a noun or a verb?

1. The film has lots of special <u>effects</u>. *noun*

2. That was the <u>effect</u> I wanted. *noun*

3. These changes <u>affect</u> everyone. *verb*

4. Tiredness <u>affects</u> your work. *verb*

Write the correct spelling.

5. forbiden *forbidden*

6. rebelious *rebellious*

7. bagage *baggage*

> **PART B Focus**
> **1–4:** near homophones; word class
> **5–7:** rules for adding suffixes
> **8:** suffixes to form adjectives
> **9–10:** synonyms; word meanings

8. Add the same suffix to make the words into adjectives.

   quarrel *some*   tire *some*   fear *some*

Underline the word that is **not** a synonym.

9. disappointed   disheartened

   <u>disposed</u>   discouraged

10. discontented   displeased

    dissatisfied   <u>displayed</u>

C Sentence work

Draw a line to show how the underlined words are used in the sentence.

Joe had seen Lucy put <u>her</u> book away so he knew <u>this</u> must be <u>his</u>.

1. her ———————— pronoun

2. this ———————— possessive pronoun

3. his ———————— determiner

> **PART C Focus**
> **1–3:** identifying determiners, pronouns and possessive pronouns
> **4:** starting sentences with subordinating conjunctions; commas
> **5–7:** expanded noun phrases
> **8–10:** uses of commas

4. Write a sentence starting with the conjunction **before**.

   Before you answer, think carefully about the question.

Write an expanded noun phrase to describe or define these different types of bird.

5. **emu**   *a large flightless bird with a long neck*

6. **owl**   *a nocturnal bird of prey with large eyes and a hooked beak*

7. **kingfisher**   *a bright blue bird with a long sharp beak*

Add the missing comma and explain why it is needed.

8. The survivors were cold, wet and terrified. *To separate the adjectives in a list of three.*

9. After they have laid their eggs, the female turtles return to the water. *To separate a fronted adverbial.*

10. "Can you see anything, Rosy?" asked Jake. *To separate the name.*

X **DEFINITIVE ANSWER**   X **SAMPLE ANSWER**

A Warm-up

Complete the noun phrase.

1. an __occasional__ shower __of light rain__
2. an __eventful__ day __at school__
3. a __new__ cover __for the book__
4. the __longest__ river __in Europe__

Write a sentence using the words **the**, **a** and **no** as determiners.

5. __The man had a long beard but no hair.__

Underline the word that is wrong. Write it correctly.

6. His voice was a little <u>horse</u>.   __hoarse__
7. I saw <u>raindeer</u> on the roof.   __reindeer__
8. Use flour to make a <u>doe</u>.   __dough__

Underline the odd one out.

9. finish   final   finalist   <u>finery</u>

10. Explain your answer.

   __It doesn't belong to the same word__
   __family.__

PART A Focus
1–4: noun phrases; use of a, an, the
5: determiners
6–8: homophones
9–10: word families

B Word work

Add the same ending to all three words.

er ing ed

1. begin __ner__   prison __er__   listen __er__
2. gossip __ing__   gallop __ing__   kidnap __ping__
3. develop __ed__   overlap __ped__   worship __ped__

Add the correct spelling of the ending to make a noun.

4. **admit**   __admission__
5. **collide**   __collision__

Add the suffixes to complete the nouns.

6. The little prince spent his child __hood__ in a faraway king __dom__ .

7. As a punish __ment__ , the prison __ers__ had no free __dom__ .

Write the meaning of the word in **bold**.

8. in a **halting** voice
   halting: __hesitating__

9. in an **argumentative** mood
   argumentative: __keen to quarrel__

10. She held it **possessively**.
   possessively: __wanting to keep it__

PART B Focus
1–3: rules for adding suffixes; exceptions
4–5: words ending ssion, sion
6–7: noun suffixes
8–10: inferring word meaning from word structure

C Sentence work

Rewrite the sentence so that both adverbials come at the start.

1. The sun came out eventually, just as we reached the summit.
   __Eventually, just as we reached the summit, the sun came out.__

2. Magnus left his house in the early hours when all was silent.
   __In the early hours, when all was silent, Magnus left his house.__

Write a two-clause sentence starting with the noun.

3. **Darkness** __fell as they reached the sea.__
4. **Gardeners** __must protect their plants when it is cold outside.__

Underline the word that is wrong. Write it correctly.

5. The dragon was asleep in <u>it's</u> cave.   __its__
6. Katie listened to the others' poems before she read <u>her's</u>.   __hers__
7. "<u>Who's</u> shoes are these?" asked Jack's mother.   __Whose__

PART C Focus
1–2: fronting adverbials; commas
3–4: sentences with more than one clause
5–7: correcting misuse of apostrophes
8–10: pronouns for cohesion and to avoid repetition

8. Underline the pronouns in the second sentence.

   Foods contain vitamins. <u>These</u> are important because <u>they</u> help children to stay healthy.

Why are the pronouns used? Give two reasons.

9. __To avoid repeating the word 'vitamins'.__   10. __To link the two sentences.__

A Warm-up

Add an adverbial to the start and end of the sentence.

1. In the morning, they begin to climb despite the threat of bad weather.

2. That evening, they returned home without any food.

Add the missing letters to make three words that mean very ugly.

3. g r o t e s q u e   g r u e s o m e
   h i d e o u s

> **PART A Focus**
> **1–2:** adding adverbials; commas after fronted adverbials
> **3:** spelling patterns
> **4–6:** homophones
> **7–10:** suffixes

Write two homophones.

4. **road**   rode   rowed

5. **he'll**   heel   heal

6. **rain**   rein   reign

Add the same suffix to make a word for someone's occupation.

7. chem ist

8. cycle ist

9. violin ist

10. dent ist

B Word work

Look at the spelling of the words below. Underline the odd one out.

1. adventurous   <u>courageous</u>   continuous

2. Explain why it is the odd one out.

   Because it keeps the 'e' on the end of the root word.

3. Complete the word sum.

   outrage + ous = outrageous

Write a noun formed from the word in **bold**.

4. **fail**   failure

5. **require**   requirement

6. **simple**   simplicity

> **PART B Focus**
> **1–3:** adding ous; exceptions
> **4–6:** suffixes to form nouns
> **7:** spelling patterns
> **8–10:** shades of meaning in synonyms

7. Add the missing letters.

   banq u e t   bouq u e t   boutiq u e

Write two verbs to describe

8. **eating greedily**   gobbling   guzzling

9. **eating noisily**   gnawing   chomping

10. **eating carefully**   nibbling   pecking

C Sentence work

Write the following as direct speech. Use the correct punctuation and a new line each time the speaker changes.

Come down from there shouted Sebastian. It's dangerous. I'm looking for something replied Joe. What are you looking for asked Sebastian. Just something muttered Joe. Something I've lost.

1. "Come down from there!" shouted Sebastian. "It's dangerous."

2. "I'm looking for something," replied Joe.

3. "What are you looking for?" asked Sebastian.

4. "Just something," muttered Joe. "Something I've lost."

Complete the sentence by adding suitable pronouns.

5. The guide led them down the corridor and they followed her .

6. I gave him my phone when he asked for it but then he said that it was his not mine .

7. When it is threatened, the puffer fish makes its body swell up and its spikes stand on end.

Complete these similes.

8. The wires were twisted like spaghetti.

9. Blossom fell like snowflakes.

10. He prowled like a tiger.

> **PART C Focus**
> **1–4:** writing and punctuating direct speech
> **5–7:** using pronouns and possessive pronouns
> **8–10:** composing similes

Ⓧ **DEFINITIVE ANSWER**   Ⓧ **SAMPLE ANSWER**

A Warm-up

Write different types of sentence using the word **question**.

1	**statement**	A question ends with a question mark.
2	**question**	What question did you ask him?
3	**command**	Ask me a question.
4	**exclamation**	What a silly question!

Add the missing letters.

Clue: word classes

5 d e t **e** r m i n e **r**

6 p r e p o s i **t** i o n

7 c o n j u n c **t** i o n

PART A Focus
1–4: types of sentence
5–7: word classes; spelling
8–10: spelling patterns

Write the correct spelling.

8	flurishing	flourishing
9	encuragement	encouragement
10	nurishment	nourishment

B Word work

Cross out the incorrect word in the sentence.

1 The medicine soon had an ~~affect~~ effect.

2 Did the heat affect ~~effect~~ the results?

3 The ~~affect~~ effect soon wore off.

4 Does diet affect ~~effect~~ our health?

5 Write the correct spelling.

effection   affection

acception   exception

PART B Focus
1–5: near-homophones
6–9: word structure
10: shades of meaning in synonyms

Write the root word and the suffix.

6	stupid	+	ity	=	**stupidity**
7	cave	+	ity	=	**cavity**
8	hostile	+	ity	=	**hostility**
9	able	+	ity	=	**ability**

Write three verbs to show different speeds of walking.

10	**slow**	saunter	stroll	amble
	quick	march	stride	pace

C Sentence work

Underline the prepositions.

1 **He rode <u>into</u> town <u>on</u> a horse <u>with</u> no name.**

2 Write another sentence using the same prepositions.

He rode into the village on a motorbike with huge handlebars.

PART C Focus
1–2: identifying and using prepositions
3–5: checking capital letters and misuse of apostrophes
6–7: expanding noun phrases to describe
8–10: Standard English pronouns

Write the noun phrases correctly.

3	the rio olympic's	the Rio Olympics
4	king arthurs castle	King Arthur's castle
5	Anglo-saxon invasion's	Anglo-Saxon invasions

Write a sentence about the given subject. Start with a descriptive noun phrase.

6	**castle**	The ancient castle on the mountain crag loomed over the village.
7	**feet**	Two scaly green feet with yellow claws were sticking out of the cave.

Add the missing pronoun **I** or **me**.

8 In class, Jess sits behind Molly and me .

9 Alex and I are going swimming tomorrow.

10 Mrs Adams says Jacob and I can work together.

Ⓧ **DEFINITIVE ANSWER**   Ⓧ **SAMPLE ANSWER**

A Warm-up

Complete the sentence after the adverbial.

1. To his astonishment, everyone stood up and began to clap.

2. In amazement, he stared at the alien.

3. Confused by all the noise, he did not know which way to go.

Add the suffix.

4. **Italy** + an = Italian

5. **Egypt** + ian = Egyptian

6. **Rome** + an = Roman

PART A Focus
1–3: sentences with fronted adverbials
4–6: noun suffixes; capital letters
7–9: shades of meaning in synonyms
10: spelling

Write a word that means

7. **very surprising** astounding

8. **really hate** detest

9. **very small** minute

10. Add the missing letters to spell words that mean **brave**.

fear less   hero ic   vali ant

B Word work

Add the suffix to make the words into adverbs.

1. **feeble** feebly

2. **drastic** drastically

3. **true** truly

PART B Focus
1–3: adding ly; exceptions to rules
4: homophones
5–7: adding suffixes to change word class
8–10: inferring word meaning from word structure

Add the correct verb.

4. sowing **seeds**   sewing **on buttons**

Add a suffix to the word in **bold** to make the word that completes the sentence.

5. He was a **king** without a kingdom .

6. He thanked his **friends** for their friendship .

7. She paid her membership fee to become a **member**.

Write the meaning of the word in **bold**.

8. **deforestation** when forests are cut down or burnt

9. **classification** when things are put into categories

10. **indentations** small marks or dents

C Sentence work

Anna Sewell started to write 'Black Beauty' when she was 50 years old.

Reorder the sentence above. Do it in two different ways.

1. When she was 50 years old, Anna Sewell started to write 'Black Beauty'.

2. Anna Sewell was 50 years old when she started to write 'Black Beauty'.

PART C Focus
1–2: reordering sentences; commas after fronted adverbials
3–5: possessive pronouns
6–7: Standard English verb forms; them/those
8–10: use and misuse of commas

Rewrite the sentence using a possessive pronoun.

3. I think that is my painting.   I think that painting is mine.

4. Those are your shoes over there.   Those shoes over there are yours.

5. This must be their address.   This address must be theirs.

Underline the words that are not Standard English.

6. "I <u>ain't</u> seen your bag," said Louis. "<u>Weren't</u> it on the bench by <u>them</u> trees?"

7. Why have non-Standard English words been used? Because they show how someone speaks.

Write the name of the punctuation mark that could replace the arrow between these clauses.

8. We just missed the bus ➜ we were an hour late.   full stop

9. Although we waited well over an hour ➜ there was still no news.   comma

10. Save our planet ➜ do it right now.   full stop

X **DEFINITIVE ANSWER**   X **SAMPLE ANSWER**

English Skills 3 Answers

A Warm-up

Add an adverbial to the sentence.

1. I couldn't sleep <u>due to the heat</u> .
2. <u>In the summer,</u> I couldn't sleep.
3. I finished my homework <u>in ten minutes</u> .
4. <u>After tea,</u> I finished my homework.

Complete the word sum.

5. **dramatic** + ly = <u>dramatically</u>
6. **basic**   + ly = <u>basically</u>
7. **erratic**   + ly = <u>erratically</u>
8. Write a sentence using one of the adverbs.
   <u>He was behaving very erratically.</u>

> **PART A Focus**
> **1–4:** adverbials and fronted adverbials
> **5–8:** rules for adding ly; exceptions
> **9–10:** shades of meaning in synonyms

Write four adjectives to describe something that is

9. **very loud**   <u>blaring</u>   <u>thunderous</u>
                      <u>deafening</u>   <u>booming</u>
10. **very horrible** <u>disgusting</u>   <u>repulsive</u>
                      <u>odious</u>   <u>appalling</u>

B Word work

Add **ous** to make the words into adjectives.
Check that you spell them correctly.

1. **glamour** <u>glamorous</u>
2. **humour**   <u>humorous</u>
3. **vigour**   <u>vigorous</u>
4. What is unusual about the spelling?
   <u>'our' changes to 'or' when 'ous' is added</u>

Add the correct spelling of the ending to make a noun.

5. **extend** <u>extension</u>
6. **attend** <u>attention</u>
7. **expand** <u>expansion</u>

> **PART B Focus**
> **1–4:** adding ous; exceptions
> **5–7:** words ending sion, tion
> **8–9:** synonyms
> **10:** changing word class; related words

Write three verbs to describe different facial expressions that show

8. **anger** <u>glower</u>   <u>scowl</u>   <u>glare</u>
9. **pain**   <u>wince</u>   <u>flinch</u> <u>grimace</u>

10. Write words formed from the verb **decide**.
    noun   <u>decision</u>   **adjective** <u>decisive</u>
    adverb <u>decisively</u>

C Sentence work

Underline the two noun phrases in the sentences below.

1. <u>A rare bird from South Africa</u> has been spotted in <u>the local park</u>.

Rewrite the sentence twice with different noun phrases.

2. <u>An escaped tiger from the local zoo has been spotted in the town centre.</u>
3. <u>A famous film star has been spotted in the department store.</u>

> **PART C Focus**
> **1–3:** expanded noun phrases to specify
> **4:** use of exclamation marks for effect
> **5–7:** using possessive pronouns
> **8–10:** identifying and using determiners and pronouns

Why does this command end with an exclamation mark?

4. **Don't touch that!** <u>To show it is urgent.</u>

Write a sentence using the pair of possessive pronouns.

5. **his mine**   <u>That book is his and this one is mine.</u>
6. **ours theirs** <u>The green bibs are ours and the red bibs are theirs.</u>
7. **hers yours** <u>That painting is hers and this one is yours.</u>

8. Underline the determiner in the sentence and circle the pronoun.
   <u>Some</u> volcanoes are active while (others) are dormant.

Write a sentence using the word **these** as a

9. **pronoun** <u>Some apples are green but these are red.</u>
10. **determiner** <u>I like these apples best.</u>

Remind the pupil to complete Section 2 of the Progress chart on page 46 of the pupil book.

(X) **DEFINITIVE ANSWER**   X **SAMPLE ANSWER**

WRITING TASK 2

Writing task assessment sheet: Time travellers

Name: _____ Class/Set: _____

Teacher's name: _____ Date: _____

Sentence structure and punctuation

	Always/often	Sometimes	Never
A range of conjunctions is used to write sentences with more than one clause			
Adverbs, prepositions and conjunctions are used to add detail about time, place and cause			
Expanded noun phrases are used to specify and add detail			
A variety of sentence types is used			
Fronted adverbials are used			
Appropriate use of tense, including progressive and perfect forms			
Appropriate use of pronouns to avoid repetition			
Sentences are demarcated accurately with full stops, capital letters, **?** or **!**			
Commas are used in lists and after fronted adverbials			
Direct speech is punctuated correctly			
Plural **s** and apostrophe **s** are used correctly			
Apostrophes are used for contractions and possession			

Composition and effect

Features of story form are used (e.g. description of setting, use of dialogue)			
Paragraphs are used to show movements in time and place			
Adverbials are used to link events			
Varied vocabulary is used and chosen for effect			

Spelling

Knowledge of spelling patterns is applied correctly			
Longer words are correct, including endings and a range of suffixes			
Correct spelling of words that are often misspelt			
Words with prefixes are correct			
Rules for adding verb endings and suffixes are applied correctly			
Spelling of plurals is correct			
Homophones and near-homophones are correct			

Writing task summary

Completed proofreading task: The world around us

Name: _____ Class/Set: _____

Teacher's name: _____ Date: _____

Sometimes our actions have a negative ~~affect~~ _e_ffect on the nat~~ch~~^ueral world.

Garden~~n~~ers use weedkiller to kill weeds_x, but they forget weedkiller is a poison_ous ~~k~~^{ch}emical_x and can be harmful~~l~~ to wildlife.

Every day, we throw away all sorts of materⁱals. In parks and open spaces, people drop litter. ~~l~~^Litter can be extrem~~l~~^{el}ey dange^orus to birds, insects and other small ~~crechers~~ _creatures_ as they can a^cciden^{al}tly get trapped inside or sw^aollow it.

Pollu^{tio}~~sh~~un from factory^{ie}s goes strai^{gh}t into rivers or it is b^uerried_x. ~~t~~^This can be a seri^ous problem and make more tr^ouble in the fut~~cher~~^{ure}.

In the countryside, people build on open land. ~~i~~^If ma^cshines cut down trees, it can change a place dramatic^{al}ly. ~~a~~^A un^{ique}eek habitat might be dist^eroyed and animals' lives could be threaten^ed.

Proofreading task summary

Section 2 tasks summary

A Warm-up

Complete the subordinate clause.

1 The king would never be satisfied even if
   he owned all the gold in the world.

2 The king would never be satisfied while
   the dragon still lived.

Add the correct homophone to complete the two words.

3 *waist* **coat**   *waste* **paper**
4 **master** *piece*   *peace* **ful**
5 **over** *hear*   *here* **abouts**

Add the missing letters.

Clue: speech

6 d i a l o g u e   8 l e c t u r e
7 c o n v e r s a t i o n

Write two verbs that mean

9   **look quickly**   *glance*   *glimpse*
10 **look carefully** *examine*   *inspect*

> **PART A Focus**
> **1–2:** using a range of subordinating conjunctions
> **3–5:** homophones
> **6–8:** spelling patterns
> **9–10:** appropriate synonyms

B Word work

Cross out the incorrect word.

1 I accept ~~except~~ your apology.
2 Come any day ~~accept~~ except Sunday.
3 Write the meaning of

   accept *believe*   **except** *apart from*

> **PART B Focus**
> **1–3:** near-homophones
> **4–5:** tricky word endings
> **6–7:** prefixes
> **8–10:** shades of meaning in synonyms

Add the same ending to complete the three words.

4 **differ** *ent*   **rec** *ent*   **frequ** *ent*
5 **cert** *ain*   **vill** *ain*   **barg** *ain*

6 Write four words with the prefix **semi**.

   semi- *final*   semi *circle*
   semi- *detached*   semi *colon*

7 What does **semi** mean?   *half or partly*

Write five words that mean different shades of

8 **blue**   *teal*   *navy*   *cobalt*
             turquoise *sapphire*

9 **purple** *mauve*   *lilac*   *indigo*
             lavender   *plum*

10 **red**   *burgundy* *cerise*   *scarlet*
             cherry   *crimson*

C Sentence work

Underline the pronoun in the second sentence.

1 **I lied about my homework. This turned out to be a big mistake.**
2 What does the pronoun refer to?   *lying about the homework*

Underline the pronouns in the second sentence.

3 **We have grown these hyacinths. Some are blue and others are pink.**
4 What do the pronouns refer to?   *the hyacinths*

Underline the words that make the statement into a question.

5 **Did you know scowling uses more muscles than smiling?**
6 Write a question formed in the same way.   *Did you know the Earth is round?*

> **PART C Focus**
> **1–4:** pronouns for cohesion
> **5–6:** forming questions
> **7–8:** adding adverbials to the start and end of a sentence
> **9–10:** use of commas

Improve the sentence by adding adverbials to give more detail.

7 *Despite his tiredness,* **Joseph plodded on** *along the steep mountain track.*
8 *Slowly, without a word,* **Bella took a step** *towards the doorway.*

Add commas to the sentence.

9 Suddenly, with the lorry only metres away, the driver slammed on the brakes.
10 As the alarm began to wail, we ran down the staircase, along the corridor, across the hallway and out of the door.

X DEFINITIVE ANSWER   X SAMPLE ANSWER

A Warm-up

Continue the sentence after the preposition.

1. I wrote a story about _a mad professor._
2. It was a story with _a happy ending._
3. There was a surprise at _the end._

Add the same letters to spell the three words correctly.

4. s u _i_ t c a s e   f r u _i_ t y   b r u _i_ s e
5. b e l _i_ e v e   a c h _i_ e v e   r e l _i_ e f

Write three adjectives to describe materials that feel

6. **very rough**   _bristly_   _coarse_   _wiry_
7. **very smooth**   _silky_   _velvety_   _glossy_

Cross out the word that is wrong. Write it correctly.

8. caravan ~~sight~~   _site_
9. mountain ~~peek~~   _peak_
10. Roman ~~freeze~~   _frieze_

> **PART A Focus**
> **1–3:** using prepositions
> **4–5:** tricky spelling patterns
> **6–7:** adjectives
> **8–10:** homophones

B Word work

Write the correct spelling of the underlined words.

1. He studied the <u>simbols</u> inside the <u>piramid</u>.
   symbols   _pyramid_
2. We are learning about <u>mussles</u> in <u>sience</u>.
   muscles   _science_
3. Ask the <u>kemist</u> about your <u>stomack</u> <u>acke</u>.
   chemist   _stomach_   _ache_

4. Add the prefix **un** to the words.
   <u>un</u> block   <u>un</u> load   <u>un</u> furl

Write a sentence using each verb with **un**.

5. _We must unblock the drains._
6. _Let's unfurl the flag._
7. _I help to unload the washing machine._

> **PART B Focus**
> **1–3:** applying spelling patterns
> **4–7:** prefixes with verbs
> **8–10:** using a dictionary to check word meanings

Use a dictionary to check the meaning of the word in **bold**. Write your own definition.

8. a **mundane** life   _ordinary_
9. he is **gullible**   _easily fooled_
10. he was **distraught**   _very upset_

C Sentence work

1. Underline the subject of the sentence.

   <u>Cows</u> eat grass.   <u>The elephant</u> drank all the water.   <u>We</u> collected the money.

> **PART C Focus**
> **1–4:** subject of a sentence
> **5–8:** future tense references
> **9–10:** checking misuse of apostrophes with plural s for possession

Add the subject of the sentence.

2. _The scientist_   found a solution to the problem.
3. _The judges_   announced the results.
4. _Spiders_   eat flies and other small insects.

Complete these predictions about your future.

5. Tomorrow, _I will get up early._
6. Later this week, _I will go to the cinema._
7. Later today, _I will watch my favourite programme on television._
8. Next week, _I will work harder._

Check the use of apostrophes. Underline words that are wrong and write them correctly.

9. The <u>dogs ear's</u> pricked when they heard the clip clop of a <u>horses'</u> hooves.   _dogs' ears_   _horse's_
10. We heard <u>peoples voice's</u> from inside <u>James</u> house.   _people's voices_   _James's_

X DEFINITIVE ANSWER   X SAMPLE ANSWER

A Warm-up

Write a sentence using the word in **bold** as a determiner.

1 **this**   This porridge is too hot.

2 **six**   I need six egg boxes.

3 **several**   I made several attempts.

Underline the word that does not belong to the same word family.

4 **capture   captive   <u>captain</u>   captivity**

5 Explain your answer.

Because it does not have a
meaning linked to being captured.

Write the correct spelling.

6 **furrious** furious   7 **magicly** magically

Complete the word to spell an adjective that means **funny**.

8 **h i l** arious

9 **h u m** orous

10 **c o m** ical

PART A Focus
1–3: determiners
4–5: word families
6–10: words ending ous, ical

B Word work

Add the suffix **able**.

1 enjoy able   value able
   agree able   comfort able

Use the words you have made in these phrases.

2 a   comfortable   armchair

3 an   enjoyable   day out

4 a   valuable   diamond ring

5 a pleasant and   agreeable   man

PART B Focus
1–5: words ending able
6–9: choosing more adventurous words
10: more prefixes: non

Write a more adventurous word to use in place of the adjective in **bold**.

6 the **brave** knight   valiant

7 the **noisy** child   boisterous

8 a **lonely** building   secluded

9 a **fancy** pattern   elaborate

10 Add the same prefix to all these words.

non sense   non stop

non -fiction   non -smoking

C Sentence work

Rewrite the sentence adding a subordinate clause.

1 **The classroom was empty.**   Although it was 9 o'clock, the classroom was empty.

Is the comma used correctly? Put a tick or a cross.

2 **A week went by, then news came at last.**   ✗

3 **He felt his stomach churning, his hands shaking and his heart thumping.**   ✓

4 Write the incorrect sentence correctly.
   A week went by. Then news came at last.

Add the word needed to complete the sentence.

5 **A bus is a large vehicle**   that   **carries passengers.**

6 **A surgeon is a doctor**   who   **does operations.**

7 Underline the pronouns in the sentence below.
   <u>She</u> bought <u>him</u> an ice cream and got <u>one</u> for <u>herself</u> as well.

PART C Focus
1: adding subordinate clauses
2–4: use and misuse of commas (between main clauses)
5–6: using who and that as conjunctions
7–10: using different types of pronoun

Write a sentence using the pronouns in **bold**.

8 **they themselves**   They found themselves in the middle of a forest.

9 **I myself**   I shall have to water the plants myself.

10 **you yourself**   You can try making this yourself.

 **✗ DEFINITIVE ANSWER   ✗ SAMPLE ANSWER**

A Warm-up

Write a sentence using the verb.

1 **flown**   All the birds have flown away.

2 **spoken**   I have spoken to my teacher
              about my homework.

3 **done**   I have done the washing up.

Write three words that start with this spelling pattern.

4 **s y m** pathy

5 **s y m** metry

6 **s y m** bol

> **PART A Focus**
> **1–3:** perfect form of verbs
> **4–6:** i sound spelt y
> **7–8:** verb choice; spelling
> **9–10:** shades of meaning in synonyms

Write two verbs that could complete the sentence.

7 Stop fi_____.   fidgeting   fiddling

8 He tr_____ home.   trudged   traipsed

Write a word that means

9 **a bit scared**   unsettled

10 **very scared**   terrified

B Word work

Add the correct suffix.

> **PART B Focus**
> **1–4:** more suffixes; rules for adding suffixes
> **5:** word classes
> **6–8:** antonyms in context
> **9–10:** spelling patterns

ive ist

1 **decorate** + ive = decorative

2 **extreme** + ist = extremist

3 **relate** + ive = relative

4 **style** + ist = stylist

5 Which of the words is an adjective that fits in this phrase?

   a   decorative   wallpaper

Write an antonym for the crossed-out word.

6 a price ~~increase~~   decrease

7 a ~~negative~~ response   positive

8 I need to ~~download~~ this video.   upload

Write the correct spelling of the underlined words.

9 He prefered going for a walk to more
   enerjetic exersise.

   preferred   energetic   exercise

10 There are picturesk views in spectacqular
   senery.

   picturesque   spectacular   scenery

C Sentence work

Write the next three sentences. Start each sentence with a time adverbial to link the events.

The tower of boxes was complete but it seemed very unsteady.

1 For a moment, it seemed that the tower would stand.

2 Then suddenly, it began to wobble and topple.

3 Within seconds, the tower had collapsed with boxes scattered everywhere.

Complete the sentence using a pair of adverbs.

> **PART C Focus**
> **1–3:** using time adverbials to link a sequence of sentences
> **4–6:** using adverbs to modify adverbs
> **7–8:** determiners
> **9–10:** writing and punctuating direct speech

4 He drove extremely carefully.

5 He spoke rather nervously.

6 The servant returned almost immediately.

Underline the determiners in the sentence below.

7 **Several trees separated our garden from the open playing field.**

8 Write other determiners that could be used instead.   six   their   an

Jess asks her teacher a question about the Romans and her teacher replies. Write this as direct speech.

9 "Mr Roberts, why did the Romans build so many roads?" asked Jess.

10 "Well," said Mr Roberts, "the roads meant their soldiers could march more quickly."

X DEFINITIVE ANSWER   X SAMPLE ANSWER

A Warm-up

Write the next three sentences.

Simon began to run up the hill.

1. At first, he found it easy.
2. Halfway up, he began to slow down.
3. When he reached the top, he was exhausted.

Underline the word that is wrongly spelt.

4. exclusion   excursion   <u>expresion</u>   extension
5. session   <u>ocassion</u>   mission   passion
6. Write the two underlined words correctly.

   expression   occasion

Add the letter to make a word family.

7. s c e n e   s c e n e r y
   s c e n i c   s c e n a r i o

Add the suffix to complete the adjective.

8. fashion able   clothes
9. protect ive   clothing
10. water proof   jacket

PART A Focus
1–3: adverbials to link sentences
4–6: words ending sion, ssion
7: spelling patterns; word families
8–10: suffixes to form adjectives

B Word work

Add the suffix **ous** to form adjectives. Check that you spell them correctly.

1. **monster**   monstrous
2. **disaster**   disastrous
3. **wonder**   wondrous

PART B Focus
1–3: rules for adding ous; exceptions
4–7: using a dictionary to check spellings; alphabetical order
8–10: prefixes with verbs

Write the correct spelling of these words. You can use a dictionary.

4. misrable   miserable
5. milleneum   millennium
6. miricle   miracle
7. Write the words in alphabetical order.

   millennium   miracle   miserable

8. Underline the prefix in the verbs.

   <u>re</u>decorate   <u>re</u>build   <u>re</u>organise

9. How does the prefix change the verbs?

   It means to do it again.

10. Write three more verbs using the same prefix.

    reorder   reheat   recycle

C Sentence work

1. Write a sentence using the noun in **bold** as the subject of the sentence.

   chef   The chef prepared a delicious meal.
   satellite   The satellite orbits the Earth.

PART C Focus
1: subject of a sentence
2–4: references to future time
5–7: proofreading; checking punctuation
8–10: using who to add information about a person

Rewrite the sentence to be about the future.

2. There are many visitors here.   There will be many visitors here.
3. It is dark now.   It will be dark soon.
4. The train is now arriving.   The train will be arriving in five minutes.

Proofread the text. Correct the punctuation.

5. Early the next day, ~~I~~n the chill morning, he set off. ᴬall the streets were empty.
6. As she opened the box, she gasped, "It's a microscope. ᴴhow wonderful!"
7. Benjamin said, "People's houses were flooded and farmers' crops destroyed."

Continue these sentences to say who the person is.

8. They took the book to Mr Anderson, who is the head teacher.
9. They went to see Jack, who worked on the farm.
10. Our reporter spoke to Agnes Wilson, who is the owner of the shop.

Ⓧ **DEFINITIVE ANSWER**   Ⓧ **SAMPLE ANSWER**

A Warm-up

Add an adverb.

1. It was _extremely_ dark inside.
2. Bob was _rarely_ late.
3. I was feeling _quite_ hungry.
4. It is _rather_ cold today.

> **PART A Focus**
> 1–4: adverbs modifying adjectives
> 5: suffixes to form adjectives
> 6–7: punctuating direct speech
> 8–10: spelling patterns

5. These words and suffixes are mixed up. Write them correctly.

   massable **photograph**ive **question**ic

   photographic   _massive_   _questionable_

Max asked Joe the time and Joe answered him. Write this as direct speech.

6. _"What time is it?" asked Max._
7. _Joe replied, "It's ten o'clock."_

Add the missing letters to make words that mean **great** or **amazing**.

8. s e n s _ational_
9. s p e c _tacular_
10. t r e _men_ d _ous_

B Word work

Write the correct spelling of these fruits. You can use a dictionary.

1. nectarene _nectarine_
2. pomegranite _pomegranate_
3. clementene _clementine_

4. Add the suffix **able** to form adjectives.

   rely _iable_   forgive _able_
   forget _table_   respect _able_

5. Write the root word.

   apologise _apology_
   flatten _flat_
   circulate _circle_

> **PART B Focus**
> 1–3: using a dictionary to check spellings
> 4: words ending **able**; rules for adding suffixes
> 5–9: verb suffixes
> 10: adventurous vocabulary

Use one of the words to complete the sentence.

6. _Flatten_ the clay with your hand.
7. I must _apologise_ for the noise.
8. Blood _circulates_ round the body.
9. What sort of words have you used? _verbs_
10. Write a more adventurous adjective.

    After the rain, the pitch was soggy.

    saturated

C Sentence work

"We mustn't let them get away," shouted Evie, racing round the corner.

Give two reasons why commas are needed in the sentence above.

1. _To separate the spoken words from the non-spoken words (shouted Evie)._
2. _To separate the 'ing' clause that adds an action after the direct speech._

> **PART C Focus**
> 1–3: commas in direct speech
> 4–5: present and past perfect form of verbs
> 6–10: forming questions using question tags; commas and question marks

3. Write another sentence using two commas in the same way.

   "I'm right behind you," said Robbie, _climbing onto his bicycle._

Write the sentence using the present perfect and past perfect forms of the verb.

4. I saw him before.   _I have seen him before._   _I had seen him before._
5. He rang the bell.   _He has rung the bell._   _He had rung the bell._

6. Underline the words that make the statement into a question.   You will help, <u>won't you?</u>

Make the statements into questions in the same way.

7. Rashid is going out.   _Rashid is going out, isn't he?_
8. Ibrahim has seen the garden.   _Ibrahim has seen the garden, hasn't he?_
9. Jack can go to the cinema.   _Jack can go to the cinema, can't he?_
10. Marie went to town on Saturday.   _Marie went to town on Saturday, didn't she?_

Ⓧ DEFINITIVE ANSWER   Ⓧ SAMPLE ANSWER

A Warm-up

Write a sentence using the word **after** as a

1 **preposition** I'll meet you after school.

2 **conjunction** I felt better after I took
the medicine.

Add the same short word to complete the three words.

3 b r e a the   s u n b a the   s o o the

4 i m p o r t ant   d i s t ant   h e s i t ant

Write two words starting with these letters.
You can use a dictionary.

5 w e i ght   w e i rd

6 r h y me   r h y thm

7 f a u lt   f a u lty

PART A Focus
1–2: prepositions and conjunctions
3–4: words that are often misspelt
5–7: spelling patterns; using a dictionary
8–10: suffixes to form nouns

Add a suffix to form a noun to complete the sentence.

8 Friend ship   is very important.

9 I'll make an except ion   for you.

10 I need an electric ian   to fix the light.

B Word work

Write the root word and suffix.

1 argue + ment = **argument**

2 explain + ation = **explanation**

3 persuade + sion = **persuasion**

4 Add the missing ending.

ary ery

ordin ary   libr ary   diction ary

mis ery   gall ery   batt ery

Add the suffix **ity** to form a noun.

PART B Focus
1–3: adding suffixes to root words; exceptions
4: words that are often misspelt
5–7: rules for adding suffixes: ity
8–10: using a dictionary to check word meanings

5 **mobile**   mobility

6 **pure**   purity

7 **stupid**   stupidity

Check the meaning of the verb using a dictionary.
Write a sentence using the verb correctly.

8 **exaggerate** His stories exaggerate what
really happened.

9 **excavate** They began to excavate
the site.

10 **exasperate** I sometimes exasperate
my teacher.

C Sentence work

Write a sentence starting with the pronoun.

1 **anyone**   Anyone can come and visit the gardens when they are open.

2 **everyone**   Everyone in my class can swim at least 10 metres.

3 **nobody**   Nobody spoke when the music ended.

4 **somebody**   Somebody has been in the kitchen and stolen the cakes.

Add the missing comma.

PART C Focus
1–4: using different types of pronoun
5–6: commas with fronted adverbials and question tags
7–10: adverbs to comment or show the writer's viewpoint

5 It's a lovely day today, isn't it?

6 To start the engine, turn the key.

7 Why is an adverb used in this sentence?

Sadly, someone has pulled up plants in the new garden.

To show that the writer thinks this is a sad thing to have happened.

Complete these sentences about the same incident.

8 **Fortunately,** most of the plants have survived.

9 **Unfortunately,** we will need to replant one area.

10 **Clearly,** we will have to make the garden more secure.

 **X** DEFINITIVE ANSWER   **X** SAMPLE ANSWER

A Warm-up

Complete the different types of sentence using the word **girl**.

1. **question** What is that girl's name?

2. **exclamation** What a clever girl!

3. **statement** That girl lives next door.

4. **question** That girl is clever, isn't she?

> **PART A Focus**
> **1–4:** sentence types (grammatical patterns)
> **5–7:** rules for adding ly
> **8–10:** antonyms in context

Complete the sentence with an adverb formed from one of the words in **bold**.

frantic chaotic manic

5. He ran frantically.

6. He tidied away manically.

7. Everything was arranged chaotically.

Write an antonym of the words in **bold**.

8. We were **best friends**. worst enemies

9. I needed to **speed up**. slow down

10. **Fortunately**, the play was a **success**.
Unfortunately failure

B Word work

Write two verbs beginning with each prefix.

1. **dis**   disappear   disagree

2. **mis**   misbehave   misspell

3. **re**   reorder   rethink

Add the same ending to these words.

4. experi ence   differ ence   sequ ence

Add **able** or **ible** to complete the word.

5. poss ible   horr ible   terr ible

6. respect able   avoid able   remark able

Use a dictionary to write the meaning of the nouns in **bold**.

> **PART B Focus**
> **1–3:** using prefixes with verbs
> **4:** tricky word endings
> **5–6:** words ending able, ible
> **7–10:** using a dictionary to check word meanings

7. **haven**   a safe place

8. **commotion**   a lot of noise

9. **pursuit**   a chase

10. Use one of the nouns to complete each sentence.

It is a   haven   for wildlife.

I'm in   pursuit   !

What a   commotion   !

C Sentence work

Write the next three sentences.

Many people would benefit from a new library.

1. For example, older people would be able to use the computers there.

2. However, it would be expensive to build.

3. Clearly, it is an important decision.

Add a phrase between the commas to say who the person is.

> **PART C Focus**
> **1–3:** using adverbials to link ideas and aid cohesion
> **4–7:** use of commas to mark information added to a sentence
> **8–10:** checking pronouns, verbs, tense

4. Mrs Singh, our head teacher, is a very kind person.

5. Ivan, the farmer's son, sat in the sunshine.

6. Megan Matthews, our next-door neighbour, enjoys dancing and singing.

7. Simon, a retired police officer, was taken to Morton Hospital.

Check the grammar. Cross out words that are wrong. Write the correct words.

8. Alfie and Joe both wanted to play the game but ~~he says~~ it ~~were~~ his turn.   Joe   said   was

9. Amy should ~~of~~ met Ben after school but ~~Amy forgets Amy's~~ promise.   have   she   forgot   her

10. Jack and Indira ~~was~~ late but ~~we~~ still ~~find~~ time to chat.   were   they   found

A Warm-up

Complete the sentence using adverbials to give more descriptive detail.

1 Under heavy skies, waves crashed in anger on jagged rocks.

Cross out the word that is wrong. Write it correctly.

2 ~~sowing~~ machine sewing

3 ~~plane~~ flour plain

4 blue ~~die~~ dye

Write another word to replace the adverb.

5 I am very cross. extremely

6 He is often cheerful. frequently

7 He is sometimes late. occasionally

Write a word belonging to the same word family.

8 **famine** famished

9 **fame** famous

10 **family** familiar

PART A Focus
1: adverbials; comma after fronted adverbial
2–4: homophones
5–7: adverbs
8–10: word families

B Word work

Write the meaning of the word in **bold**.

1 The wolf enjoyed **terrorising** sheep.
terrorising: frightening

2 It was an **electrified** fence.
electrified: with an electric charge

3 Bees help **pollinate** flowers.
pollinate: spread pollen (from flower to flower)

Write the correct spelling.

4 delishous delicious

5 caushous cautious

6 vishous vicious

PART B Focus
1–3: inferring meaning from word structure
4–6: words ending tious, cious
7–10: using suffixes to form verbs

7 Change the word into a verb by adding a suffix.

pure purify

modern modernise

straight straighten

Use each verb in one of the sentences.

8 There are plans to modernise the station.

9 Filtering helps to purify the water.

10 Stand up and straighten your legs.

C Sentence work

Extend these sentences using one of these words.

who which that

1 The two friends were so happy that they could not stop laughing.

2 She sat next to Aaron and Beth , who were always arguing.

3 They went to the shop which had just opened.

Rewrite the sentence so it begins with the adverbial.

4 They fell asleep one by one. One by one, they fell asleep.

Complete the sentence using the past perfect form of the verb.

5 **ran** I looked for him but he had run away.

6 **forgot** They tried to open the door but Dad had forgotten the key.

7 **ate** I wanted a biscuit but someone had eaten them all.

PART C Focus
1–3: using who, that and which to add information
4: fronting adverbials
5–7: past perfect forms to make time references
8–10: recognising commas, dashes, brackets

Write the name of the punctuation mark used to separate parts of the sentence.

brackets comma dash

8 It was a lovely sunny day – a perfect day for a picnic. dash

9 The parrot (called Squawk) flapped its wings. brackets

10 Mr Jenkins, the driver, started the engine. commas

Ⓧ **DEFINITIVE ANSWER** Ⓧ **SAMPLE ANSWER**

A Warm-up

Write a sentence using the pronoun.

1. **itself** — The computer switches itself off.

2. **theirs** — That big house is theirs.

3. **something** — There is something outside.

4. **these** — I like most nuts but not these.

5. Underline the root in this word family.

   <u>cent</u>ury   per<u>cent</u>age   <u>cent</u>igrade

6. What does the root mean?   a hundred

7. Write another word belonging to the word family.

   centurion

   PART A Focus
   1–4: different types of pronoun
   5–7: roots and word families
   8–10: words ending **able/ible**

Add a suffix so the word matches the definition.

8. like **able**   pleasant and friendly
9. enjoy **able**   pleasing to do
10. flex **ible**   bendy

B Word work

Use a dictionary to check the spelling of these foods. Write the correct spelling.

1. mayonaise   mayonnaise
2. yogert   yogurt/yoghurt
3. samossa   samosa

4. Add the correct endings.

   cial tial

   spe **cial**   so **cial**   par **tial**   torren **tial**

   PART B Focus
   1–3: using a dictionary to check spellings
   4–6: words ending **cial, tial**
   7–9: antonyms; spelling
   10: adventurous vocabulary

Use the words in these noun phrases.

5. torrential rain   a special agent
6. social media   a partial success

Add the missing letters to spell the antonyms.

7. t r a n s p a r e n t   o p a **q** u e
8. p r e **c** i s e l y   v a g u **e** l y
9. m o n s t r **o** u s   g o r **g** e o u s

10. Write a word to use in place of **pulled**.

    He **pulled** the door open.   wrenched

C Sentence work

1. Underline the two adverbials that could be used to show a different opinion.

   <u>however</u>   moreover   therefore   also   <u>on the other hand</u>   finally

Complete the next sentence.

2. The holiday is expensive. **However,** it will be worth it.
3. The holiday is expensive. **Also,** we will need spending money when we get there.
4. The holiday is expensive. **Therefore,** I shall have to save up my money.

Add the determiners.

5. He needed an X-ray and an injection.
6. Many boats use the River Thames every day.

Add the missing commas.

7. Mrs Lucas, the head teacher, was not very pleased.

8. How did you know where to put the commas?

   They separate the extra information added to the sentence.

   PART C Focus
   1–4: adverbials to link ideas and build cohesion
   5–6: determiners; use of a/an
   7–10: using commas to add information to a sentence

Write another two sentences using commas in this way.

9. Charlie Jackson, my next-door neighbour, is really funny.
10. Adam Miles, the baker, won first prize.

X DEFINITIVE ANSWER   X SAMPLE ANSWER

A Warm-up

Add adverbials to say where and when.

1 As the day dawned, _____ land was sighted _____ through the sea mist.

2 After twenty years, _____ the prisoner escaped _____ from the island.

Add a suffix to make the verb into a noun.

3 **occupy** _____ occupation

4 **satisfy** _____ satisfaction

5 **intend** _____ intention

PART A Focus
1–2: adding adverbials to the start and end of sentences
3–5: suffixes to form nouns
6–10: words ending **able**

Underline the word you cannot add **able** to.

6 wash   drink   break   <u>mess</u>   read

Add **able** to the other words above. Use each adjective you make in a sentence.

7 This jumper is washable.

8 The tap water is drinkable.

9 Glass is very breakable.

10 This book is very readable.

B Word work

Write a definition of the verb.

1 **memorise**   to learn by memory

2 **equalise**   to make equal

3 **supervise**   to be in charge of

Add two suffixes or verb endings to the word.

4 **limit**   limited   limitation

5 **permit**   permitted   permission

6 **forbid**   forbidden   forbidding

Underline the word that is wrongly spelt. Write the correct spelling.

7 treasure   pleasure   <u>leasure</u>   measure
    leisure

8 forward   <u>aukward</u>   downward   eastward
    awkward

PART B Focus
1–3: verb suffixes; inferring meaning from word structure
4–6: rules for adding suffixes; exceptions
7–8: words that are often misspelt
9–10: challenging vocabulary

Underline the word not often used today. Write its meaning.

9 He struck the door <u>thrice</u>.   three times

10 They travelled from <u>afar</u>.   a distance

C Sentence work

I was just about to put the fish in the net when I dropped it.

Explain why the sentence above could be confusing.

1 Because the pronoun 'it' could refer to the fish or the net.

PART C Focus
1–2: checking pronouns for ambiguity
3–4: expanded noun phrases
5–7: adverbs to show writer's point of view
8–10: use of dash for effect/between clauses

2 Write the sentence so the meaning is clear.

I dropped the fish when I was just about to put it in the net.

Write a longer noun phrase.

3 a cheese **sandwich** on brown bread   4 the most famous **paintings** in the art gallery

Write in a suitable adverb to show that the writer is not happy.

5 Unhappily, _____ there was no choice.   7 Unfortunately, _____ they made a mistake.

6 Clearly, _____ I will be writing to complain.

8 Why has a dash been used in this sentence?   **Did he fall – or was he pushed?**

To give a dramatic pause between the two clauses.

Draw an arrow to show where a dash could go in these sentences.

9 We had to do something→and do it fast!

10 Everything was fine→until the rain started.

X **DEFINITIVE ANSWER**   X **SAMPLE ANSWER**

A Warm-up

Lava flows from the volcano when it erupts.

Write the word that is used as a

1 **preposition** from   3 **pronoun** it

2 **conjunction** when   4 **determiner** the

5 Rewrite the sentence above so it begins with the subordinate clause.

When it erupts, lava flows from the volcano.

Write the meaning of the word in **bold**.

6 a **multistorey** car park

multistorey: it has many levels

7 Write two words that begin with the same prefix.

multicoloured   multimedia

8 What does this prefix mean?   many

PART A Focus
1–4: identifying word classes
5: fronting subordinate clauses; commas
6–8: meaning of prefixes
9–10: spelling patterns

Add the missing letters.

9 a r m o u r   t o u r i s m   h o n o u r

10 s a u s a g e   a u b e r g i n e   s a u c e

B Word work

Write the root word.

1 multiplication   multiply

2 evaporate   vapour

3 publicity   public

PART B Focus
1–3: word structure; root words and suffixes
4: adding **ation**; exceptions
5–6: using a dictionary to check spellings when needed
7–10: challenging language; idioms

4 Add **ation**. Check that the spelling is correct.

despair   desperation

Cross out words that are wrongly spelt. Write the correct spellings. You can use a dictionary.

5 I saw ~~peaces~~ of gold and ~~preshous jewells~~.

pieces   precious   jewels

6 ~~Emralds~~, rubies, ~~dimands~~, sapphires and ~~cristals~~.

emeralds   diamonds   crystals

What do these phrases mean?

7 she's in hot water   she's in trouble

8 he cried his eyes out   he cried a lot

9 keep your hair on   stay calm

10 give me a hand   help me

C Sentence work

Complete the next two sentences. **The boy fell asleep in the sun.**

1 Fortunately, he was wearing a sunhat.

2 Unfortunately, someone stole his hat while he was sleeping.

Write a sentence using the three prepositions.

3 **along during over**   During the night, the cat prowled along the fence and over the rooftops.

4 **behind between in**   In a panic, I dodged behind the wall and squeezed between the railings.

Complete the sentences.

I think an after-school club is a great idea.

5 Firstly, it gives children a chance to socialise with their friends.

6 Secondly, it helps parents who are working.

7 Thirdly, you can use the time to complete homework.

Add the other bracket into the sentence.

PART C Focus
1–2: adverbs to comment on events
3–4: using prepositions
5–7: using adverbials to link ideas
8–10: using brackets

8 Mount Everest (the tallest mountain in the world) is in the Himalayas.

9 **Billy:** (*standing up*) Follow me, everyone.

10 The two elephants (Ella and Bella) have been moved to a new enclosure.

Remind the pupil to complete Section 3 of the Progress chart on page 46 of the pupil book.

X DEFINITIVE ANSWER   X SAMPLE ANSWER

Writing task assessment sheet: Escaped tiger causes chaos

Name: _____ Class/Set: _____

Teacher's name: _____ Date: _____

Sentence structure and punctuation

	Always/often	Sometimes	Never
A range of conjunctions is used to write sentences with more than one clause (including **who**, **that**)			
Adverbs, prepositions and conjunctions are used to add detail about time, place and cause			
Expanded noun phrases are used to specify and add detail			
A variety of sentence types is used			
Fronted adverbials are used			
Appropriate use of tense, including perfect forms or references to future time			
Appropriate use of pronouns to aid cohesion and avoid repetition			
Sentences are demarcated accurately			
Commas are used in lists and after fronted adverbials			
Inverted commas are used for direct quotes			
Apostrophes are used for contractions and possession			

Composition and effect

Features of a newspaper are used (e.g. lead sentence, quotes)			
Paragraphs are used to develop events			
Adverbials are used to link ideas and events			
Varied and adventurous vocabulary is used and chosen for effect			

Spelling

Knowledge of spelling patterns is applied correctly			
Longer words are correct, including suffixes and endings			
Correct spelling of words that are often misspelt			
Words with prefixes are correct			
Rules for adding verb endings and suffixes (and exceptions) are applied correctly			
Spelling of plurals is correct			
Homophones and near-homophones are correct			

Writing task summary

Completed proofreading task: In the dark

Name: _____   Class/Set: _____

Teacher's name: _____   Date: _____

On Friday night's, I usally stay at aunt Jane's house. On this patiqular
[u above usally, A above aunt, O corrects On, r c above patiqular]

occassion, aunt Jane was upstares looking for a travel broshure when suddenly
[A above aunt, irs above upstares, c above broshure]

all the lights went out.

I herd aunt Jane shouting frantikly from the bedroom.
[a above herd, A above aunt, cal above frantikly]

"James, are you okay?"she called. "What's happend? Do we need an electrishan?"
[e above happend, ci above electrishan]

"I'm fine," I shouted back, trying to make my way to the frunt door
[o above frunt]

without bumping into the furnitcher.
[ure above furnitcher]

when I looked outside, it was obveously not just our house with no
[W corrects when, i above obveously]

electrisity. all the houses had been plunged into darkness accept number six.
[c above electrisity, A corrects all, ex above accept]

something pekquliar was happenning. how intrigeing!
[S corrects something, c above pekquliar, H corrects how, u above intrigeing]

what was that mistereous glow coming from number six? I was cureous to
[W corrects what, y i above mistereous, i above cureous]

disscover more.

Proofreading task summary

```



```

Section 3 tasks summary

```




```

Full list of Schofield & Sims English Skills books

Pupil books

English Skills Introductory Book	ISBN 978 07217 1402 8
English Skills 1	ISBN 978 07217 1404 2
English Skills 2	ISBN 978 07217 1406 6
English Skills 3	ISBN 978 07217 1408 0
English Skills 4	ISBN 978 07217 1410 3
English Skills 5	ISBN 978 07217 1412 7
English Skills 6	ISBN 978 07217 1414 1

Answer books

English Skills Introductory Book Answers	ISBN 978 07217 1403 5
English Skills 1 Answers	ISBN 978 07217 1405 9
English Skills 2 Answers	ISBN 978 07217 1407 3
English Skills 3 Answers	ISBN 978 07217 1409 7
English Skills 4 Answers	ISBN 978 07217 1411 0
English Skills 5 Answers	ISBN 978 07217 1413 4
English Skills 6 Answers	ISBN 978 07217 1415 8

Teacher's Guide

The teacher's guide contains the **Entry tests**, **Diagnostic checks** and many other useful items suitable for use with the **English Skills** pupil books:

English Skills Teacher's Guide	ISBN 978 07217 1416 5

Also available

Mental Arithmetic is similar in format to **English Skills**, providing intensive maths practice.

For further information about both series, visit the Schofield & Sims website (www.schofieldandsims.co.uk).

Free downloads

A range of free downloads is available on the Schofield & Sims website, including:

- **National Curriculum chart**
- **Entry tests**
- **Entry test group record sheet**
- **Entry test marking keys**
- **Selecting the appropriate pupil book**
- **Achievement award certificates.**